Credits

Publisher
Roland Elgey

Publishing Manager
Lynn E. Zingraf

Editorial Services Director
Elizabeth Keaffaber

Managing Editor
Michael Cunningham

Director of Marketing
Lynn E. Zingraf

Acquisitions Editor
Martha O'Sullivan

Product Development Specialist
John Gosney

Technical Editor
C. Herbert Feltner

Technical Support Specialist
Nadeem Muhammed

Production Editor
Kathryn J. Purdum

Book Designers
Barbara Kordesh
Ruth Harvey

Cover Designers
Dan Armstrong
Kim Scott

Production Team
Tammy Ahrens
Debra Kincaid
John Ley
Pete Lippincott
Tom Missler
Linda Quigley
Holly Wittenberg

Indexer
Ginny Bess

Composed in *Syntax* and *New Century Schoolbook* by Que Corporation

We'd Like to Hear from You!

As part of our continuing effort to produce books of the highest possible quality, Que would like to hear your comments. To stay competitive, we *really* want you, as a computer book reader and user, to let us know what you like or dislike most about this book or other Que products.

You can mail comments, ideas, or suggestions for improving future editions to the address below, or send us a fax at (317) 581-4663. For the online inclined, Macmillan Computer Publishing has a forum on CompuServe (type **GO QUEBOOKS** at any prompt) through which our staff and authors are available for questions and comments. The address of our Internet site is **http://www.mcp.com/que** (World Wide Web).

In addition to exploring our forum, please feel free to contact me personally to discuss your opinions of this book: I'm **104436, 2300** on CompuServe, and I'm **jgosney@que.mcp.com** on the Internet.

Although we cannot provide general technical support, we're happy to help you resolve problems you encounter related to our books, disks, or other products. If you need such assistance, please contact our Tech Support department at 800-545-5914 ext. 3833.

To order other Que or Macmillan Computer Publishing books or products, please call our Customer Service department at 800-835-3202 ext. 666.

Thanks in advance—your comments will help us to continue publishing the best books available on computer topics in today's market.

John Gosney
Product Development Specialist
Que Corporation
201 W. 103rd Street
Indianapolis, Indiana 46290
USA

About the Author

Jennifer Fulton is a self-taught veteran of computing—which means that if there's something that can happen to a computer user, it's happened to her. Jennifer brings what's left of her sense of humor along with her vast experiences to each of her books, including the *10 Minute Guide to Excel 97, The Complete Idiot's Guide to FrontPage, Netscape Navigator 6-in-1, The Big Basics Book of the Internet,* and *The Big Basics Book of Windows 95.* Jennifer and her husband Scott (another computer book author) live in a new home filled with many books, some of which they have not written.

Acknowledgments

This time around, I got to work with some new folks, and wonderful ones they turned out to be! Special thanks to John Gosney and Katie Purdum. So good to meet you! I'd also like to thank Martha O'Sullivan, who helps more than she knows.

Trademarks

Contents

Part III: Adding Clip Art to Your Slides — 93

Part IV: Creating an Organization Chart — 119

Part V: Working with Tables — 137

Contents

Introduction

What You Can Do with PowerPoint

Microsoft PowerPoint is a fun and easy-to-use presentation graphics program. You use a presentation graphics program to create informative displays that can highlight new corporate products or services, or update others on progress toward a common goal. A PowerPoint presentation can contain charts, artwork, tables, and organizational charts, as well as special effects and sounds.

Instead of displaying your work on pages (as a word processor does), PowerPoint displays your work on the screen as *slides*. You can view one or many slides on your monitor at the same time. And when you finish your presentation, you can display it on a standard-size computer monitor or a large projection monitor, or you can print it out in a variety of ways.

PowerPoint provides all the tools you need to create a beautiful presentation with a minimum of effort: professionally designed backgrounds, pre-formatted page layouts, and wizards that guide you step by step through different processes. The following list gives you an overview of the things you can do with the powerful PowerPoint features:

- *Use toolbar buttons to perform common tasks.* Although you can still use menu commands, most of the tasks you perform often are just a mouse click away! The Standard and Formatting toolbars are always visible and contain buttons for the most common commands.

- *Choose a beautiful background using design templates.* Create a presentation with attractive background designs that look like the work of a professional graphic artist. Each background (or design template) contains colors, patterns, and a design scheme that gives your presentation continuity as well as a professional look.

- *Use different types of slide layouts.* As you're creating your presentation, you may find that you want different types of information on your slides. PowerPoint contains a variety of AutoLayouts—slides that already contain a title, graphics, charts, bulleted lists, or any combination of these, layed out in an attractive design.

- *Enter text easily.* You can add text to a slide easily by clicking the "Click to add text" box that contains preformatted text styles. When you click this box, a text box appears. You enter your text in the box, and you can edit, delete, or add to the text at any time.

- *Change bullet symbols.* You can enter text on a slide as a bulleted list in which a symbol precedes each line of text. (You can even change the symbol if you want.)

- *Format type and paragraphs.* PowerPoint provides preformatted text styles that look professional and attractive. In addition, you can change the typeface (font), type size, alignment, and other attributes to enhance and personalize your text.

- *Check your spelling.* Make sure you spelled the words in your presentation correctly using the spell checking utility. PowerPoint even enables you to add your own words to the dictionary.

- *Create an organizational chart.* An organizational chart—or org chart, for short—is a great addition to any slide. You can add, delete, and move people within the chart, as well as change the display style of groups.

- *Add a table to your presentation.* Using PowerPoint's Insert a Microsoft Word Table button, you can take advantage of Word's incredible table capabilities. You can create a table that has multiple columns and rows, and you can format the table using the Table AutoFormat feature.

- *Illustrate your data using a chart.* You can add a chart to your presentation to illustrate complex data. For example, you could add a chart showing the amount of sales over a given period. You can change the chart style to suit the data you wish to present, such as a pie chart, or a line chart.

- *Use WordArt to make your text stand out.* The WordArt feature enables you to apply special effects to text—such as making words look wavy or stretched. In addition, you can change colors and add shadow effects to your WordArt.

- *Use the Drawing toolbar to make your point.* With the Drawing toolbar, you can add arrows, circles, and other shapes to enhance various parts of your presentation. You can even draw on a slide while giving your presentation, if you like.

- *Create Speaker's Notes, Meeting Minutes, and Action Items.* PowerPoint's Meeting Minder feature enables you to create Speaker's Notes, which you can use during your presentation to remind yourself of things you want to mention. Meeting Minutes are the slide-by-slide comments you make on the presentation. Action Items are important points that you need to give attention to when the presentation is over. Once the presentation ends, you can print out and distribute the contents of the Meeting Minder. At that time, the Action Items list of actions you plan to take (which you created during the presentation) is compiled on a new final slide.

- *Print your presentation.* You can print your presentation in a variety of ways. You can print slides on a color or black and white printer with one slide per page or with many miniature slide images on a single page. You can even print each slide on a transparency if you want to use your presentation on an overhead projector.

- *Create a slide show to display on a computer.* You can show your slides on a computer for others to see. When you do, you can apply special effects such as sounds, animations, and transition effects to give your presentation a professional quality.

About the Program

This book covers Microsoft PowerPoint for Windows 97. With this book, you'll learn how to start the PowerPoint program from the Windows 95 Start menu, as well as from the Microsoft Office 97 toolbar. (The Office 97 suite includes Word for Windows, Excel, Access, Outlook, Binder, and PowerPoint. However, you do not have to install the entire Office 97 suite of programs on your computer in order to use this book.)

However, some of the tasks within this book will only work if you do have certain Office programs installed. For example, Tasks 46 through 52 teach you how to create and manage a Word table within PowerPoint. You cannot perform these tasks unless Word for Windows is installed on your computer.

Task Sections

The Task sections include the steps for accomplishing a certain task (such as adding a new slide or checking spelling). The numbered steps walk you through a specific example so that you can learn the task by actually doing it.

Big Screen

At the beginning of each task is a large picture of your PC screen showing the results of the task or some other key element from the task (such as a menu or dialog box).

Inserting a Chart on a Slide

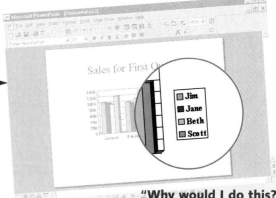

"Why would I do this?"

Each task includes a brief explanation of why you would benefit from knowing how to accomplish the task.

"Why would I do this?"

A chart presents data in a graphical format so that people are better able to see trends in data and pick up on the point you are making. By turning numeric data into a chart, you can make the data (and your audience) come alive. And when you use a chart on a slide, you don't have to worry about your numbers being small and illegible—as they often are in traditional (boring) presentations.

Step-by-Step Screens

Each task includes a screen shot for each step of the procedure. The screen shot shows how the computer screen looks at each step in the process.

Task 53: Inserting a Chart on a Slide

1 In Slide View, open the slide on which you want to insert a chart. Click the **Insert Chart** button. PowerPoint opens a datasheet (table), which you use to enter your chart data and create the chart.

Missing Link
The terms, *table* and *datasheet* are interchangeable.

2 The data displayed in the datasheet is fake—it's there so you can see how to enter your own data correctly (by simply following the example). When you enter data into each cell (box) it replaces the sample data. Click on the cell that contains the word, "1st Qtr," and type the name of a category. Press the **right arrow** to move to the next cell. Continue until you've entered all your categories.

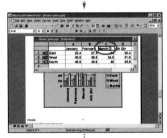

Missing Link Notes

Missing Link notes tell you a little more about the procedure. For example, these notes may define terms, explain other options, refer you to other sections, or provide hints and shortcuts.

Puzzled? Notes

The Puzzled? notes tell you how to undo certain procedures or how to get out of unexpected situations.

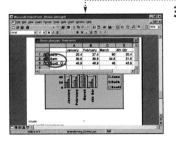

3 Click on the cell that contains the word, "East," and enter the name of your first data series. If your table contains more than one data series, press the **down arrow** to move to the cell that contains "West." Continue until you've entered all your data series names.

Puzzled?
If you're not happy with the rotated chart, click the **Undo** button on the Standard toolbar.

7

PART I

Getting Started Quickly

MICROSOFT POWERPOINT ENABLES YOU to create professional-looking presentations which can then be replayed before an audience using your computer. If you're a sales representative with a portable PC, you can create interesting presentations which will excite your audience and close the sale. If you're a manager of a large department, you can use your presentations to help summarize departmental or company-wide changes. If you're a real-estate agent, you can create colorful presentations that highlight the best features of each home listing. The uses of Microsoft PowerPoint are endless.

A PowerPoint *presentation,* consists of one or more *slides* (screens of information) that contain brief statements on which you can elaborate when you actually give your talk. With PowerPoint, you can add lots of visual effects (such as shading and color) to your slides to make them more eye-catching. In addition, you can display the data on your slides in a wide variety of ways using bulleted lists, tables, charts, and graphic images (clip art, or art you draw yourself). You can even animate your text and graphics to make them more appealing to your audience.

If a PC is not available when you need to replay your presentation before an audience (or if you don't want to use a PC), you have these options:

- You can print out your slides on a color or black and white printer.

- Using special transparency film and an ordinary Xerox machine, you can create overheads of your printouts and use them instead.

- You can save your presentation to a file which can then be made into real slides by a skilled film processor.

- Using your modem, you can give your presentation "on-line" to a co-worker located far away.

- You can even publish your presentation on the Internet, or a local *intranet* (a company-wide *Internet*work.)

As you create your presentation, you accomplish most tasks by clicking a button on a toolbar. Although there are lots of buttons and toolbars, you never have to worry about forgetting which button does what because each button has a ToolTip that tells you what it does (when you position your mouse pointer over a toolbar button, the button's name appears next to it).

To help you create your presentation, PowerPoint includes *wizards* that guide you through each step. For example, after answering a few simple questions, the AutoContent Wizard creates a series of slides that contain text based on your presentation topic! Of course, you can always modify the text if you choose.

But it's not enough for your words to sound great; your presentation has to look great, too. To make your slides look terrific, PowerPoint comes with many design templates that give your slides a uniform look, binding them together into a professional presentation. Templates not only contain professionally created colors and patterns, but also a *layout pattern*. The layout pattern determines where text and graphics are placed on a slide, along with how that text looks on the slide. You can change the layout design throughout your presentation by changing to another template; in addition, you can change the layout for an individual slide.

PowerPoint provides many views with which you can look over your presentation. In Slide view, you view only a single slide at a time. In Slide Sorter view, you can view each of your slides on-screen, as small images. In Outline view, the text on each slide is presented in outline form, allowing you to make swift changes to the order of your presentation. You'll learn how to use all these views in Part I.

In this part of the book, you will learn how to create a professional looking presentation using PowerPoint's AutoContent Wizard. Once the presentation is complete, you will add a new slide, apply a different design template, and then save and print your slides. You will also learn how to properly close PowerPoint.

Starting Microsoft PowerPoint

"Why would I do this?"

In order to use the features in Microsoft PowerPoint, you first have to turn on your computer and start the program. Once you start PowerPoint, you can open an existing presentation or create a brand new one.

How you start the program depends on whether you installed the Microsoft Office Shortcut Bar. Follow steps 1–3 if you did not install it; follow steps 4–6 if you did.

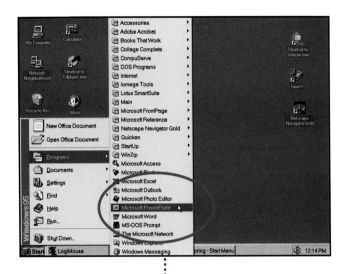

1 Click the **Start** button on the Windows 95 taskbar. The Start menu appears. Typically, Microsoft places its program items on the main Programs menu. Using your mouse, point to **Programs**, and the Programs menu appears. Move the mouse over **Microsoft PowerPoint** and click.

Puzzled?

If you mistakenly start the wrong program by clicking its name, close that program and perform step 1 again.

2 When you start Microsoft PowerPoint for the first time, you're greeted by the Office Assistant. To begin using PowerPoint, click on **Start using PowerPoint** in the Office Assistant.

Missing Link

You can learn about PowerPoint before you start using it by clicking **See key information for upgraders and new users** in the Office Assistant. You'll see a dialog box listing new features. When you've learned what you need, click **OK** and then complete step 2 to start using PowerPoint.

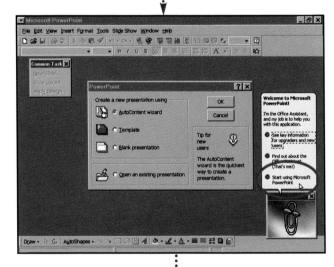

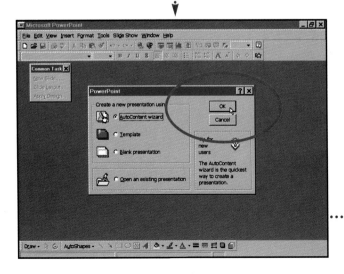

3 The PowerPoint dialog box that appears on-screen whenever you start PowerPoint enables you to open an existing presentation or start a new one. Make a selection and click **OK**. The easiest way to create a new presentation is to select AutoContent Wizard. You're now ready to start using PowerPoint. To begin, skip to Task 2.

4 If the Microsoft Office Shortcut Bar appears on your desktop. You can use it to open PowerPoint. Click the **Microsoft PowerPoint** button.

5 This PowerPoint dialog box appears each time you start PowerPoint, and it enables you to open an existing presentation or start a new one. Make a selection and click **OK**. If you'd like to create your presentation using the easiest method, then select AutoContent Wizard. You're now ready to start using PowerPoint. Proceed to Task 2. ■

Missing Link

When you work in a word processing program, you create a document that contains several pages of text. When you work in a presentation graphics program such as Microsoft PowerPoint, you create a *presentation* that contains information on *slides*.

Creating a Presentation Using the AutoContent Wizard

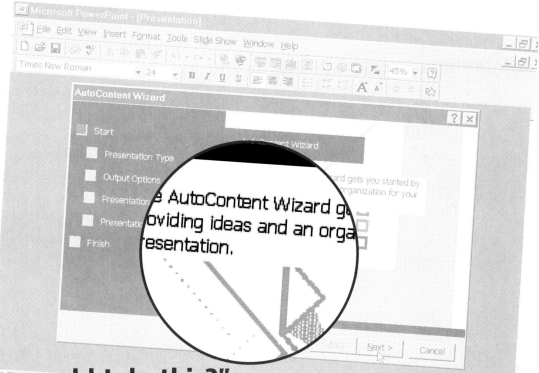

"Why would I do this?"

When you start a new presentation by selecting a template, PowerPoint creates only a single slide to start you off with. You then add slides to the presentation as needed. However, when you choose the AutoContent Wizard instead, PowerPoint provides a "semi-completed" presentation. All you do is answer a few questions telling PowerPoint what your presentation is about and how you want to present it. Then PowerPoint creates a series of slides with beautiful designs and colors, complete with placeholder text that guides you in finishing your presentation. You can change the design and modify the text to fit your taste and needs.

Task 2: Creating a Presentation Using the AutoContent Wizard

1 In the PowerPoint dialog box, the AutoContent Wizard is the default selection. (A selected option button contains a dot in the circle next to the option.) Click **OK**.

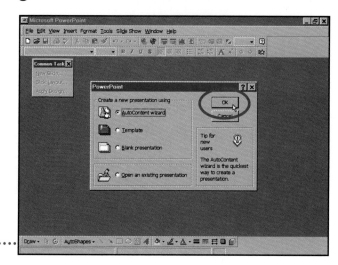

Missing Link

A dialog box option that is already selected is called the *default* selection.

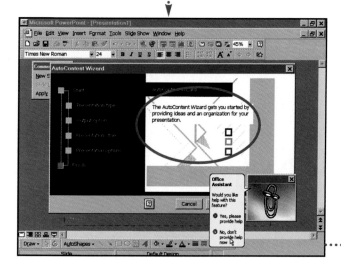

2 The Internet Wizard may appear asking if you'd like help. Click yes or no. When you return to the opening AutoContent Wizard dialog box, read it. It gives you a little information about what this wizard does and how it works. When you finish reading, click **Next>**. The Presentation Style screen appears.

3 On the Presentation Style screen, you click on the **Corporate** which fits the type of presentation you want to give. For example, click the Corporate button. A listing of corporate-related topics appears. Click on one of these topics to select it, such as **Financial Overview**. When you finish selecting your topic, click **Next>**. The Output Options screen appears.

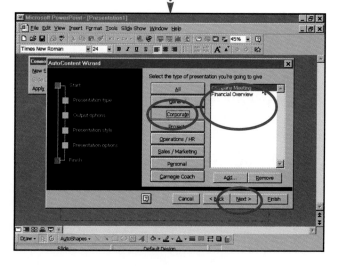

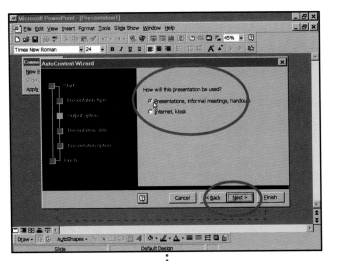

4 Here on the Output Options screen, you select how you want to present your information. Click the **Presentations, informal meeting, handouts** option. If you want your presentation to run automatically, select **Internet, kiosk**. When you're sure of the selection you've made, click **Next>**. The Presentation Styles screen appears.

Puzzled?

If you selected the Internet kiosk option in step 4, the Presentation Styles screen will *not* appear. Skip to step 7.

5 On the Presentation Styles screen, select the type of output you need for your presentation. For example, select **Color overheads**. Also, select whether or not you want to print handouts. When you're satisfied with your selections, click **Next>**. The Presentation Options screen appears.

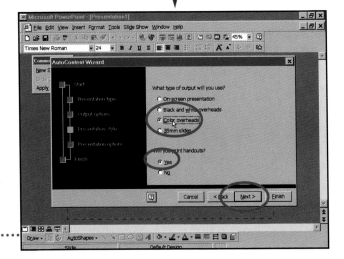

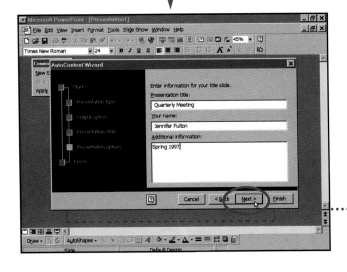

6 If you selected the Presentations, informal meeting, handouts option in step 4, then your Presentation Options screen looks like this. Enter the information you want to appear on your title slide (the first slide in the presentation). Click in each text box (such as the Your name text box) and type your information. When you're through, click on **Next>** then skip to step 8.

Task 2: Creating a Presentation Using the AutoContent Wizard

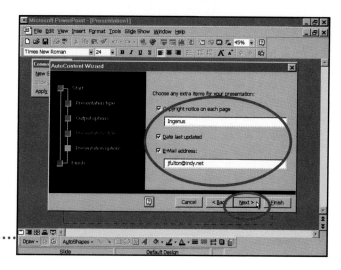

7 If you selected the Internet kiosk option in step 4, then the Presentation Options screen looks like this instead. Click an option to select it. For example, click the Copyright notice on each page option. When you're done, click **Next>**.

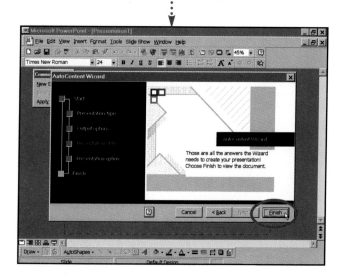

8 Click **Finish**, and PowerPoint creates a presentation based on your responses. When PowerPoint finishes creating the presentation, you see its title slide on-screen. ■

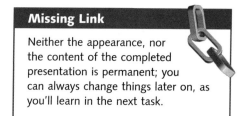

Missing Link

Neither the appearance, nor the content of the completed presentation is permanent; you can always change things later on, as you'll learn in the next task.

Replacing the Sample Text

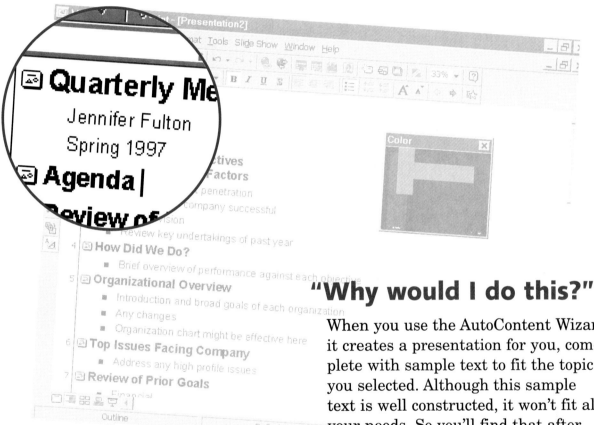

"Why would I do this?"

When you use the AutoContent Wizard, it creates a presentation for you, complete with sample text to fit the topic you selected. Although this sample text is well constructed, it won't fit all your needs. So you'll find that after reviewing the presentation that the AutoContent Wizard created, you may want to replace the text on some of the slides with something more specific.

After creating your presentation, the AutoContent Wizard will display it, using Outline view. Outline view is the easiest view to use when you want to concentrate on the *content* of your presentation, instead of its *look*.

Task 3: Replacing the Sample Text

1 The Common Tasks toolbar may appear. You can remove it from the screen by clicking its Close button. Now click at the beginning of the text you wish to replace. A view of the slide appears in the Color box.

Missing Link

When text is selected, it is highlighted in reverse colors. When you select text and then type, the selected text is replaced with new text.

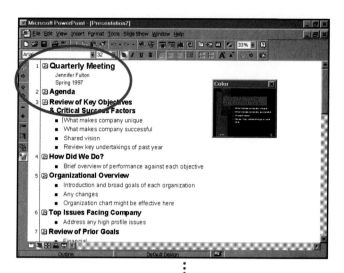

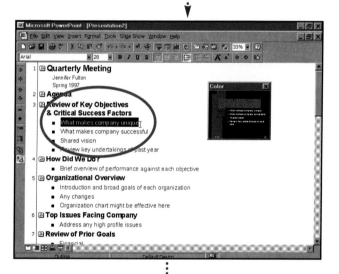

2 While holding down the mouse button, drag the pointer to the end of the text you wish to replace. The text is highlighted from the point where you clicked in step 1 to the point at which you stop dragging the mouse.

Puzzled?

If you have trouble highlighting the text you want to replace, you can repeat steps 1 and 2 as many times as you need.

3 Type the replacement text. What you type replaces the text you selected in step 2.

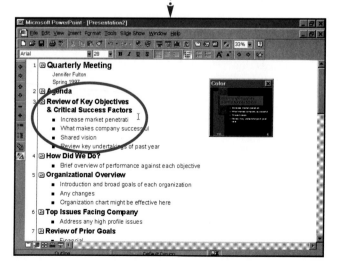

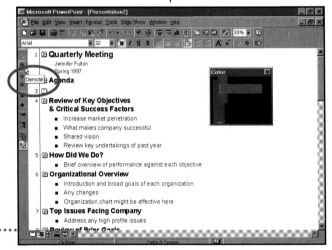

4 If you want to insert text, click at the end of the line *above* where you want to add the text and press **Enter**.

Puzzled?

When you press Enter, the line which is inserted is the same type as the line on which you clicked. For example, if you click at the end of a title line and press Enter, then a new slide (title) is inserted. If you click at the end of a bulleted list item and press Enter, then a new bulleted item is inserted.

5 To demote the text to a lower level in the outline, click the **Demote** button. For example, to change the title of a slide into bulleted text (an item in a list, preceded by a bullet—a dot—or a dash), click anywhere on the title and then click the Demote button. The slide title is changed to a bulleted item.

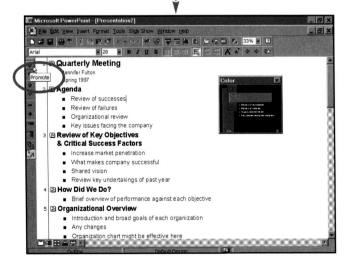

6 To promote text in an outline, click the **Promote** button. For example, to change an item in a bulleted list into a slide title, click anywhere on the bulleted list item, then click the Promote button. ■

21

TASK 4

Using the Different Views

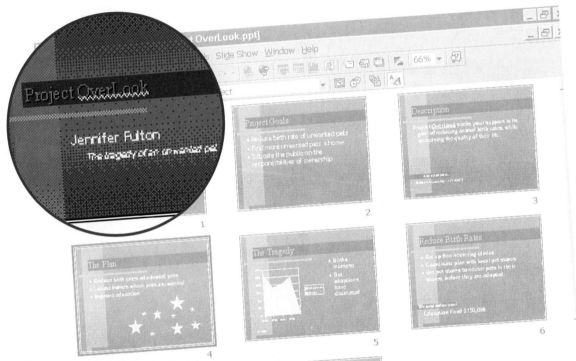

"Why would I do this?"

When you create a presentation using the AutoContent Wizard, you start out in Outline view. (The name of the view you are currently using appears in the Status bar.) Outline view is the easiest to use when dealing with presentation text. Slide Sorter view, shown here, is the one to use when you want an overview of the presentation. In Slide Sorter view, all your slides appear in miniature *thumbnails*.

As you work, you'll often switch from one view to another, in order to find a view which suits your needs at the moment. Luckily, PowerPoint has several views that show the slides (either together or separately) in varying amounts of detail.

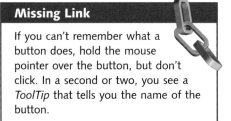

1 The icon to the left of each slide indicates if it contains any graphics. If the slide has some art, then a small picture appears in the icon. The slide view buttons in the lower-left corner of the screen enable you to change from one view to another. The button for the current view looks pushed in. Click the **Slide View** button to change to Slide view.

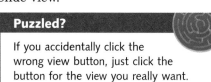

Puzzled?

If you accidentally click the wrong view button, just click the button for the view you really want.

2 In Slide View, PowerPoint displays one slide at a time. In this view you can easily read all the detail on a particular slide, so this is the view to use when adding graphics, or rearranging the data on a slide. Click the **Notes Pages View** button to change to that view.

Missing Link

If you can't remember what a button does, hold the mouse pointer over the button, but don't click. In a second or two, you see a *ToolTip* that tells you the name of the button.

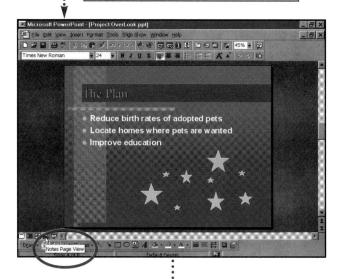

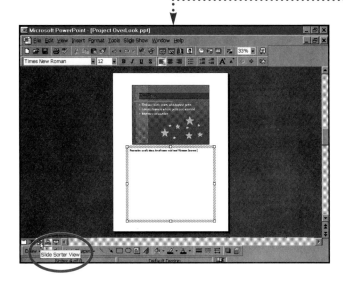

3 Notes Page View displays a miniature version of one slide per page with space for notes. Here you can add reminders about what you want to talk about when you display the slide. (Notes do not display to your audience.) Click the **Slide Sorter View** button to see all the slides in your presentation, as shown in the large figure on the previous page. ■

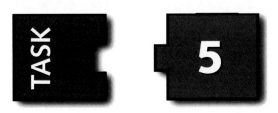

Moving from Slide to Slide

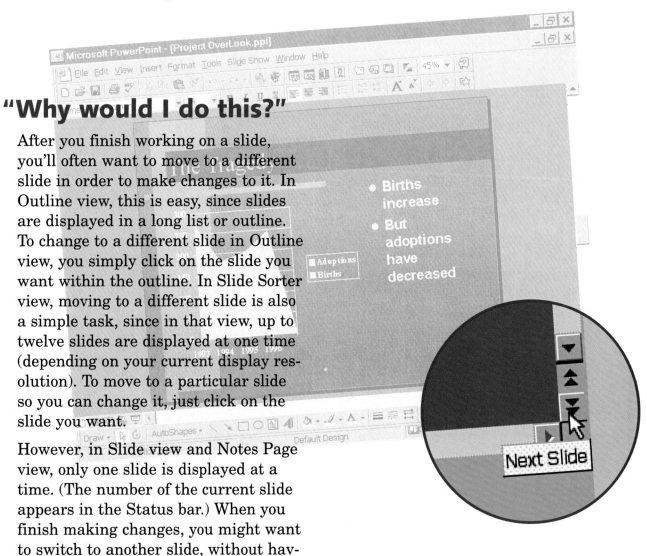

"Why would I do this?"

After you finish working on a slide, you'll often want to move to a different slide in order to make changes to it. In Outline view, this is easy, since slides are displayed in a long list or outline. To change to a different slide in Outline view, you simply click on the slide you want within the outline. In Slide Sorter view, moving to a different slide is also a simple task, since in that view, up to twelve slides are displayed at one time (depending on your current display resolution). To move to a particular slide so you can change it, just click on the slide you want.

However, in Slide view and Notes Page view, only one slide is displayed at a time. (The number of the current slide appears in the Status bar.) When you finish making changes, you might want to switch to another slide, without having to change to Outline view or Slide Sorter view. You can do that easily, as you'll see here.

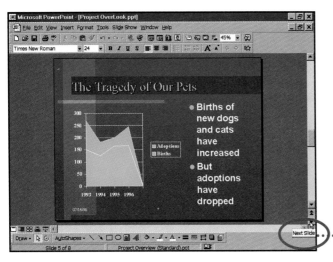

1 The steps for moving from slide to slide are the same in both Slide view and Notes Page view. To move to the next slide in the outline, click on the **Next Slide** button.

2 To move back to a previous slide, click on the **Previous Slide** button.

Puzzled?

You can click the Previous Slide button repeatedly to move backwards in the outline as far as you want. You can also click the Next Slide button as needed to move forward in the outline.

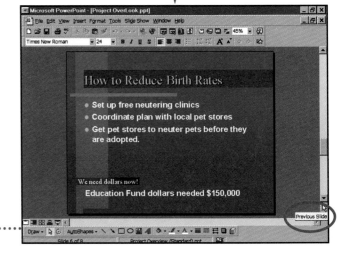

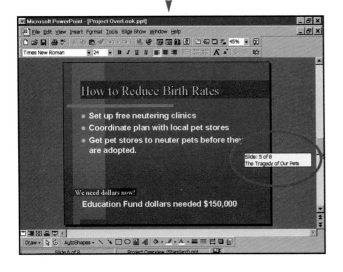

3 To move to a particular slide quickly, click and drag the scroll box in the vertical scroll bar. As you drag, a bubble appears, providing you with the exact location of each slide in the presentation. Drag the scroll box up or down until the bubble tells you that you're at the slide you want, then release the mouse button. ∎

TASK 6

Applying a Different Design Template

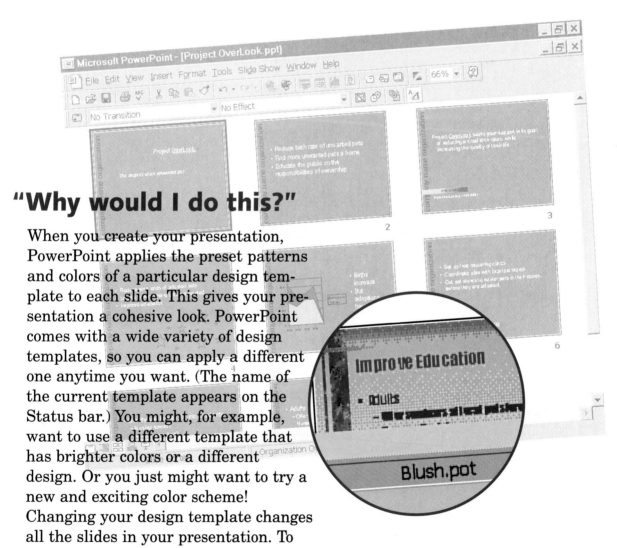

"Why would I do this?"

When you create your presentation, PowerPoint applies the preset patterns and colors of a particular design template to each slide. This gives your presentation a cohesive look. PowerPoint comes with a wide variety of design templates, so you can apply a different one anytime you want. (The name of the current template appears on the Status bar.) You might, for example, want to use a different template that has brighter colors or a different design. Or you just might want to try a new and exciting color scheme! Changing your design template changes all the slides in your presentation. To change the design for an individual slide, see the next task.

Blush.pot

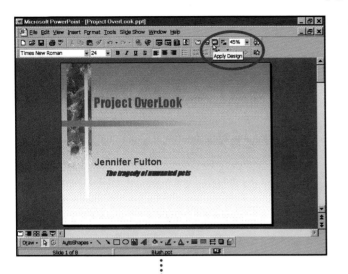

1 You can perform these steps while in any view, such as Slide **Sorter** view. Click the **Apply Design** button on the Standard toolbar. PowerPoint displays the Apply Design dialog box, open to the Presentation Designs folder, which contains a list of available color schemes.

Puzzled?

If your list of design templates looks different from the list here, you may not have all the templates installed on your computer. Reinstall Microsoft PowerPoint, and then look in the Apply Design dialog box.

2 When you click the name of a design template, a preview of it appears in the box to the right of the list. Click the name of the design template you want to use and click **Apply**.

Puzzled?

PowerPoint stores the design templates in the Presentation Designs folder. If that folder is not listed in the Look in text box, click the arrow on the Look in drop-down list and select **Presentation Designs**.

3 PowerPoint returns you to the view you were in before and applies the template's styles to all the slides in the presentation, even if they are not currently being displayed. (This will take a few minutes.) ■

Missing Link

You can also click **Apply Design** on the Common Tasks toolbar, to change your presentation's template. The Common Tasks toolbar appeared the first time you started PowerPoint; however, you can click its close button to remove it from the screen (as I did) to give you more room in which to work.

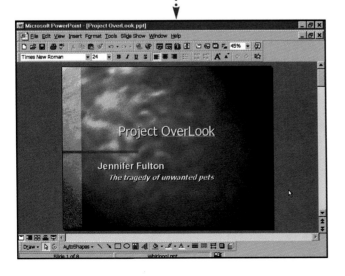

27

Applying a Different Layout to a Slide

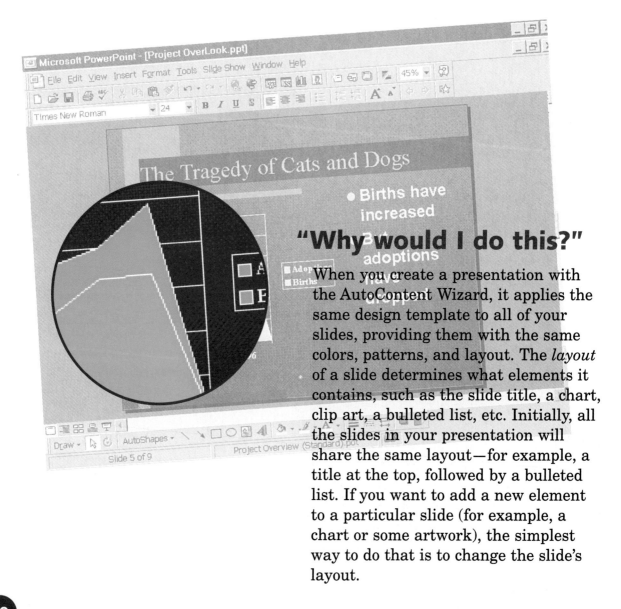

"Why would I do this?"

When you create a presentation with the AutoContent Wizard, it applies the same design template to all of your slides, providing them with the same colors, patterns, and layout. The *layout* of a slide determines what elements it contains, such as the slide title, a chart, clip art, a bulleted list, etc. Initially, all the slides in your presentation will share the same layout—for example, a title at the top, followed by a bulleted list. If you want to add a new element to a particular slide (for example, a chart or some artwork), the simplest way to do that is to change the slide's layout.

28

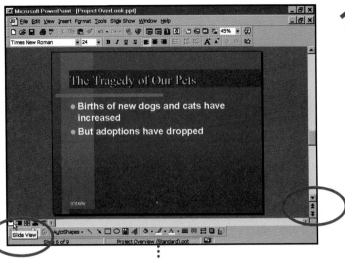

1 Change to Slide view by clicking the **Slide View** button, so you can see your slide's layout better. Click the **Previous Slide** or the **Next Slide** button on the Vertical scroll bar as needed to move to the slide whose layout you wish to change.

Puzzled?

The template controls the look of all the slides in your presentation. When you change the layout of a single slide, you change the position and type of elements it contains.

2 Click the **Slide Layout** button on the Standard toolbar. The Slide Layout dialog box appears. You can also click **Slide Layout** on the Common Tasks toolbar, which appeared the first time you started PowerPoint. (It does not appear in these figures because I clicked its close button to give me more room to work.)

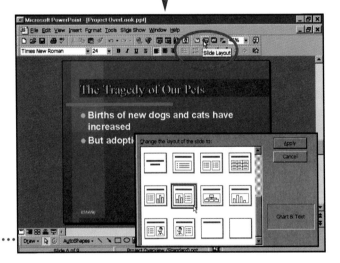

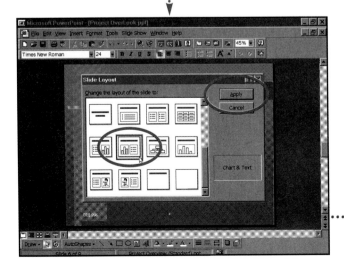

3 The slide's current layout is highlighted in blue. Click the layout you want to change to, and click **Apply**. The slide's layout changes to the one you selected.

4 To finish adding the new element such as the chart shown here, double-click on it. For example, double-click on the box which says, "Double-click to add chart." ■

Missing Link

You can also use the Slide Layout dialog box to *reapply* the current master layout of your presentation, if you want. For example, if all the slides in your presentation follow the Bulleted List layout, then click on that layout and click **Reapply**.

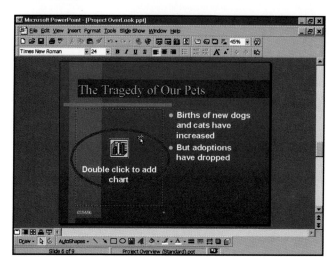

Adding a New Slide

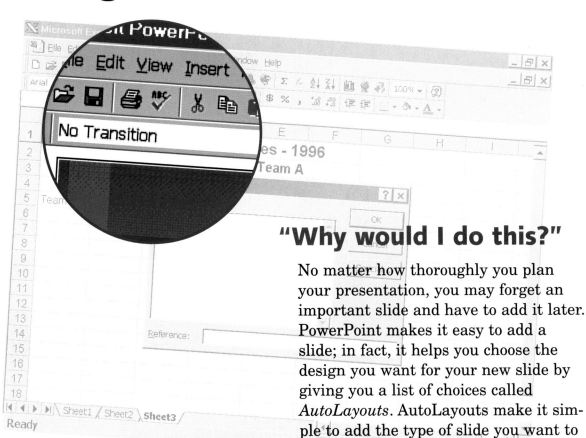

"Why would I do this?"

No matter how thoroughly you plan your presentation, you may forget an important slide and have to add it later. PowerPoint makes it easy to add a slide; in fact, it helps you choose the design you want for your new slide by giving you a list of choices called *AutoLayouts*. AutoLayouts make it simple to add the type of slide you want to your presentation. The AutoLayout determines the location of the elements on your new slide, such as the slide title, a bulleted list, a chart, clip art, etc. After using an AutoLayout to add your new slide, all you have to do to enter each element is to click (or double-click as indicated) on the appropriate area.

Task 8: Adding a New Slide

1 The slide you select is the *active* slide (it has a dark border around it). When you add a slide, PowerPoint inserts it after the active (selected) slide. In Slide Sorter View, click the slide located *before* the point where you want to insert a new slide.

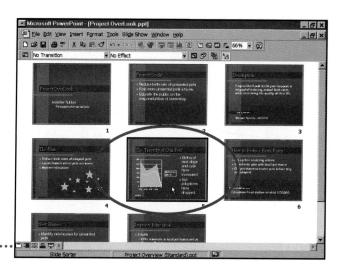

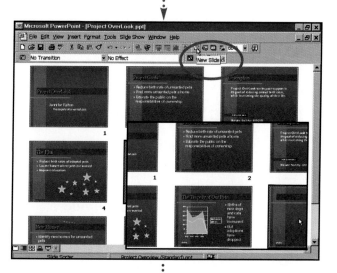

2 Click the **New Slide** button on the Standard toolbar. (You can also click **New Slide** on the Common Tasks toolbar, if it is visible.)

Puzzled?

If you insert your new slide in the wrong location, you can always move it later using Outline view. If you decide you don't want to add the slide at all, click the **Undo** button on the Standard toolbar.

3 Choose the type of slide you want to add from the list of AutoLayouts and click **OK**. In this figure, the Clip Art & Text Auto-Layout option is selected (it has a blue border around it).

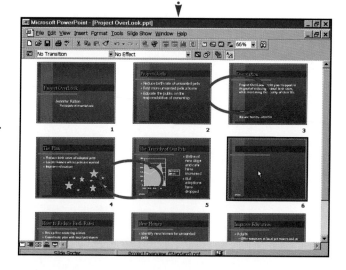

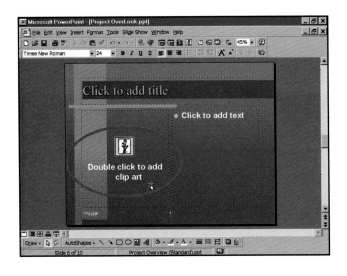

4 PowerPoint adds the new slide to your presentation *just after the slide you selected in step 1*. Placeholders appear for each element. To add an element, switch to Slide View as shown here, then click or double-click the placeholder as indicated. ■

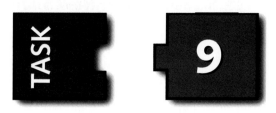

TASK **9**

Saving a Presentation

"Why would I do this?"

Few people start a project and work straight through until they finish. If you'd like to be able to work a little at a time on your presentation, you need to save it each time you stop working on it. In addition, you should resave your file as you continue to work on it, so you won't lose any of your changes.

When you save your presentation, you give it a meaningful name and indicate where you want to store it within your computer. Usually, you store it in a specific area where you keep other related work, such as other PowerPoint presentations.

1 PowerPoint displays the name of your presentation in the title bar. PowerPoint automatically calls it "PresentationX" because you have not yet saved it. To save your presentation, click the **Save** button. The Save As dialog box appears.

Missing Link

If you're going to create a presentation that's very similar to an existing one, open the existing presentation and select **File, Save As**. Enter a new name in the **File name** text box and click **Save**.

2 Type a name for your presentation in the **File name** text box. The name can include up to 255 characters, as well as spaces and punctuation. When you finish entering the name, click **Save**. You're returned to your presentation file. If you try to close your file without saving your changes, PowerPoint will remind you to do so.

Puzzled?

After you save a presentation the first time, the Save As dialog box doesn't reappear when you click the **Save** button. It only appears when you save a presentation that has not yet been named.

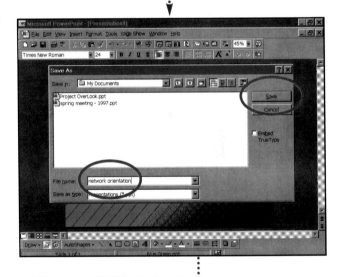

3 Although it's optional, you might want to enter important details about your presentation in the Presentation Properties dialog box. Enter the information you want to record and click **OK**. Depending on how PowerPoint is installed on your computer, this dialog box may not automatically appear. If it doesn't, PowerPoint returns you to the active slide after step 2. In that case, to display the Presentation Properties dialog, open the **File** menu and select **Properties**. Then click on the **Summary** tab. ■

35

Saving a Presentation to the Internet

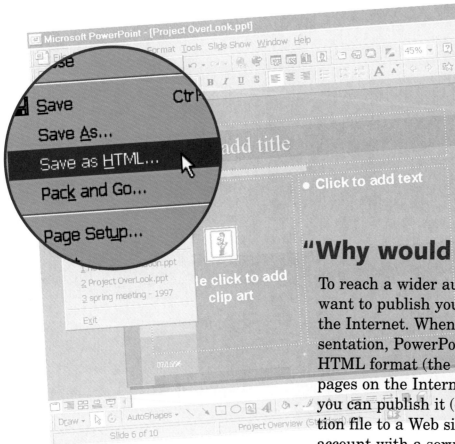

"Why would I do this?"

To reach a wider audience, you might want to publish your presentation on the Internet. When you save your presentation, PowerPoint converts it to HTML format (the format for Web pages on the Internet). At that point, you can publish it (copy the presentation file to a Web site), after opening an account with a service provider and obtaining the necessary permissions. You can also publish your presentation on a local *intranet* (a company run Internet-like network).

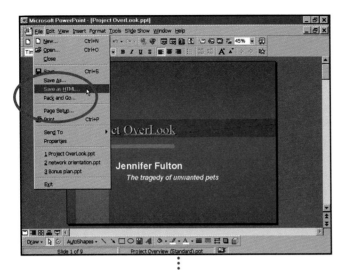

1 To save your presentation in HTML format so that it's ready to publish on the Internet, open the **File** menu and select **Save As HTML**. Then Save as HMTL dialog box appears.

Missing Link

Rather than converting your presentation to HTML so you can publish it on a Web site, you can simply copy your PowerPoint file to an FTP (File Transfer Protocol) site for others to download to their systems.

2 If this is first time you've used this command, the Internet Assistant will appear Save As HTML. The dialog box contains many screens from which you'll make your selections. After reading the introduction, click **Next>** to move to the Layout selection screen.

Puzzled?

While making your selections, you can return to a previous screen at any time by clicking the **<Back** button.

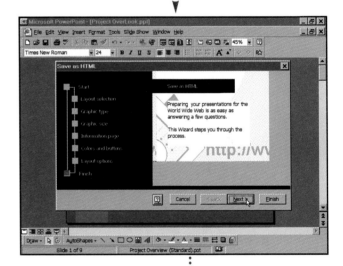

3 If you've created an HTML layout before, you can reuse it by selecting from the Load existing layout list. To create a new HTML layout, click **New layout**. Click **Next>** to move to the page style screen.

Puzzled?

After making your selections in the Save as HTML dialog box, you'll save them in a layout which you can reuse.

4 If you'd like to use frames with your Web site, click **Browser frames**. Otherwise, click **Standard**. Click **Next>** to move to the Graphic type screen.

Missing Link

Frames divide a Web page into smaller sections which can be scrolled independently. Some Web browsers, however, do not support frames, so those users may not be able to view your Web site if you use them.

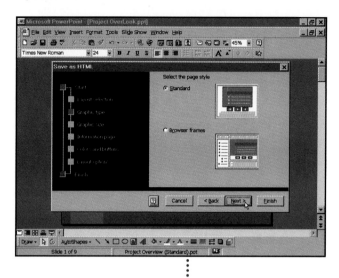

5 Select the graphic type you wish to use: GIF or JPEG. If you want to use the PowerPoint Animation Player to add animation capabilities to your Web site, select that option instead. Click **Next>** to move to the monitor resolution screen.

Missing Link

There are only two graphic formats supported by the Web: GIF or JPEG. GIF offers a smaller file size and fine quality, while JPEG offers better quality graphics.

6 Select the resolution you'd like to use at your Web site. Select also the relative size of your graphics. Click **Next>** to move to the Information page.

Puzzled?

Resolution is determined by the number of pixels (tiny dots) displayed on-screen. The resolution, 640 by 480 (640 pixels horizontally by 480 pixels vertically), has less pixels than 1280 by 1024 resolution, so it provides less detail.

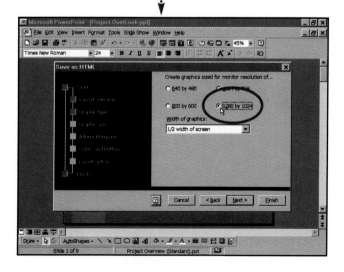

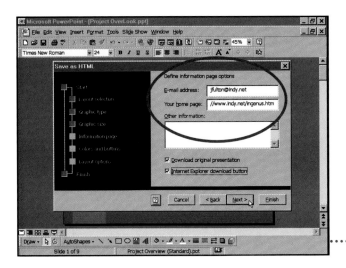

7 Enter the information you wish displayed on an Information Page, which is added to the front of your presentation. You can include your e-mail and home page addresses, as well as links to your original presentation file, and to Internet Explorer as well. Click **Next>** to move to the Colors and buttons screen.

8 Here, you can change the color of your text links, and the buttons which move a user from page to page within your Web site. For example, click **Change Text** and select a text color for your Web pages. The Link color is the color of the text which, when clicked, links the user to another Web page. Once a link is visited, its color is changed to the Visited color. Transparent buttons let the color (or graphic) used as your background show through. Click **Next>**.

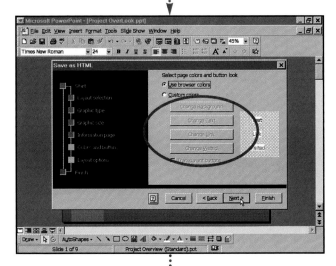

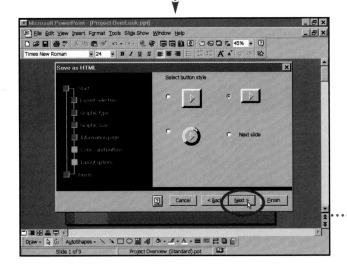

9 Select a button style and click **Next>**. These buttons appear on each Web page, and they allow the user to move through your presentation.

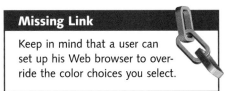

Missing Link

Keep in mind that a user can set up his Web browser to override the color choices you select.

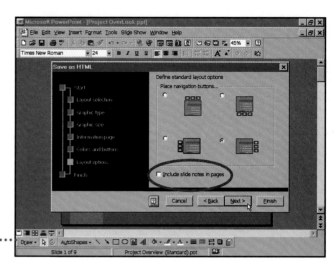

10 Select where you want the navigation buttons placed. Also, you can have your notes displayed with your presentation, by clicking the **Include slide notes in pages** option. Click **Next>**.

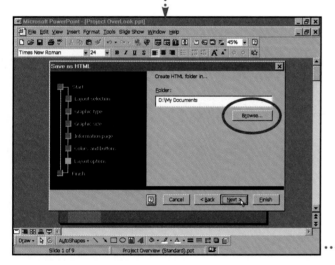

11 Select the directory into which you want the HTML version of your presentation saved. By default, PowerPoint saves it in the My Document directory. To choose a different directory, click **Browse**, select a directory from the list, and click **OK**. Click **Next>** when you're through.

12 This is the last screen. If you need to make changes to your prior selections, click **<Back** to move backwards to a previous screen. When you're ready for PowerPoint to save your presentation using your selections, click **Finish**.

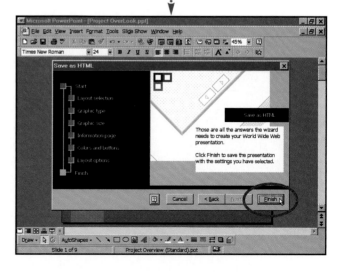

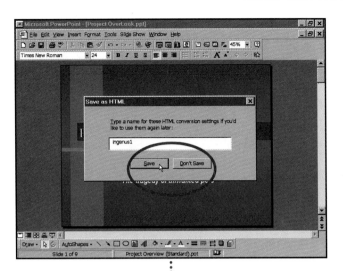

13 Enter a name for your layout and click **Save**. This allows you to reuse these same selections for another presentation later on. If you don't plan on reusing these selections, click **Don't Save**.

Puzzled?

When it comes time to publish your presentation, copy all the files you'll find in the directory you specified in step 11 to your Web site.

14 When PowerPoint is through saving your presentation, you'll see this message. Click **OK** to return to PowerPoint. ■

Missing Link

You can preview your presentation by loading it into your Web browser. For example, in Netscape, open the **File** menu, select **Open File in Browser**, then select the index.html file which you'll find in the directory you selected in step 11.

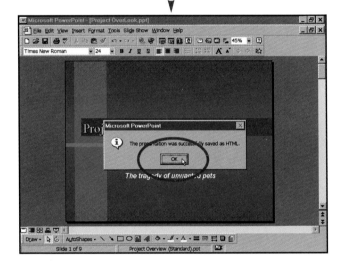

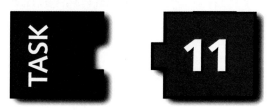

Printing a Presentation

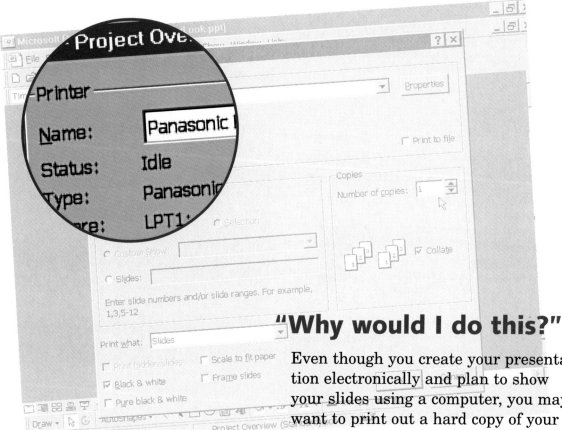

"Why would I do this?"

Even though you create your presentation electronically and plan to show your slides using a computer, you may want to print out a hard copy of your work. You can print your slides one per page, or multiple thumbnails (miniature versions of each slide) on a single page. You can then pass the hard copies on to anyone who couldn't sit in on your presentation.

In addition, you can print your notes or an outline of the text on each slide. You can use these as guides when you give your presentation.

1 Open the **File** menu and choose **Print** to access the Print dialog box, in which you can choose the type of printed materials you want.

Missing Link

If you click the Print button on the Standard toolbar (the one with the picture of a printer on it), PowerPoint automatically prints one copy of each slide.

2 Select what you want to print (slide copies, handouts, notes, or an outline) by clicking on the **Print what** drop-down arrow and selecting from the choices listed. To change the number of copies that print, change the number in the **Number of copies** box. To print the current slide only, select that option under **Print range**. You can print specific slides by typing the number of each slide in the **Slides** text box. (Separate each slide number with a comma, as in 1,3,4.)

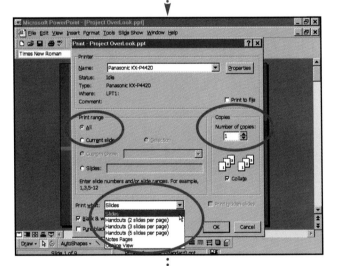

3 When you finish making your selections, click **OK**. ■

Puzzled?

You can stop a print job you've started by double-clicking the printer icon on the PowerPoint Status bar. A red X appears over the icon, and PowerPoint deletes the print job (stops it).

43

Closing a Presentation

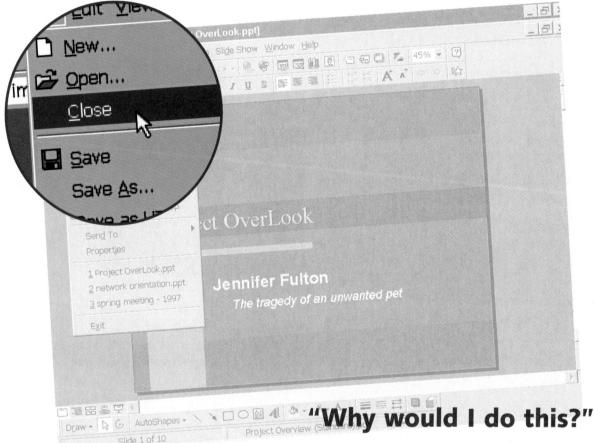

"Why would I do this?"

Closing a presentation when you finish working on it frees up memory in your computer. Your computer uses this memory to perform a variety of Windows 95 and PowerPoint tasks. The more memory available to your PC, the faster it can work. In addition, if you close a presentation after you finish with it, you won't run the risk of accidentally making changes to it.

44

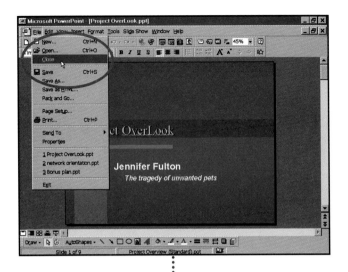

1 Open the **File** menu and choose **Close**. If you haven't made any changes to your presentation since you opened it or since the last time you saved it, PowerPoint automatically closes the file.

Missing Link

You can also click the document window's **Close** button (the X located at the right end of the menu bar.)

2 If you have made changes since the last time you saved the file, PowerPoint asks you if you want to save the changes now. Choose **Yes** to save the changes. (You can choose No to abandon the changes or Cancel to return to the presentation.)

Puzzled?

If you choose to save changes to an unnamed presentation, Power-Point displays the Save As dialog box so you can name the file.

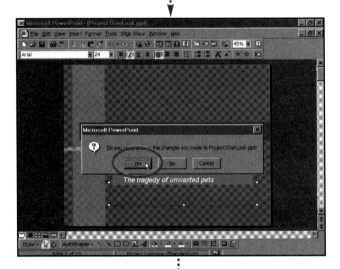

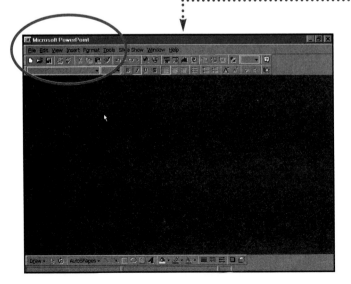

3 When PowerPoint closes your presentation, it displays a blank screen. From here, you can start a new presentation, open an existing one, or exit the program. If you see "Click to add new slide," you can click the text box to start a new presentation. ∎

Missing Link

If you have another presentation that's open, instead of seeing a blank screen, your other presentation will be displayed on-screen instead.

Starting a New Presentation

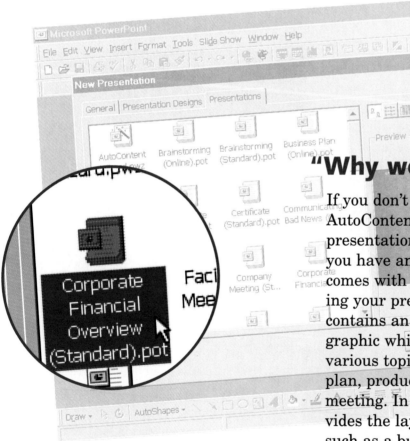

"Why would I do this?"

If you don't want to use the AutoContent Wizard to create a new presentation (as explained in Task 2), you have an alternative. PowerPoint comes with several *templates* for creating your presentation. Each template contains an attractive background or graphic which perfectly compliments various topics, such as a marketing plan, product overview, or company meeting. In addition, the template provides the layout of common elements, such as a bulleted list, or art work. PowerPoint also comes with some generic designs which easily fit many different topics. You can use any of these templates or designs as they are, or you can modify them to suit your needs.

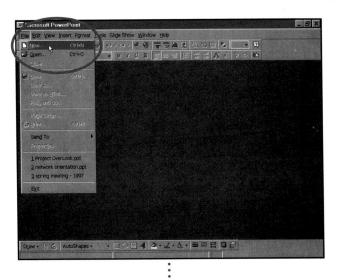

1 Open the **File** menu and choose **New** to start a new presentation. If you click the **New** button instead, it will create a blank presentation (without a background).

Puzzled?

If you don't see a template or a design you like, you can start the AutoContent Wizard from the Presentations tab. Just click the AutoContent Wizard icon in step 3, and click **OK**. PowerPoint starts the AutoContent Wizard.

2 You can start from scratch (without a design) by selecting the **Blank Presentation** icon, the General tab, and then clicking **OK**. To create a presentation with an appropriate background for your topic, click the **Presentations** tab instead.

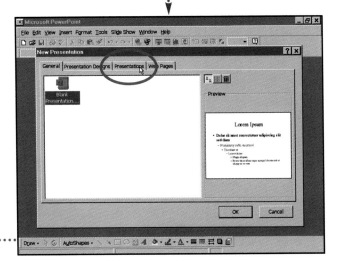

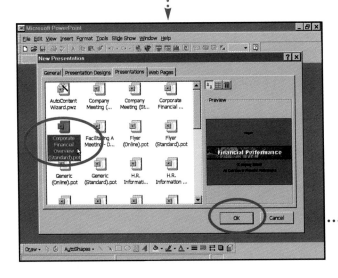

3 On the Presentations tab, click the icon for the type of presentation you want to create and click **OK**. If you want to present your data on the Internet or an intranet, select an *online* rather than a *standard* icon. When you click an icon, PowerPoint displays a preview of that presentation type on the right side of the dialog box.

Task 13: Starting a New Presentation

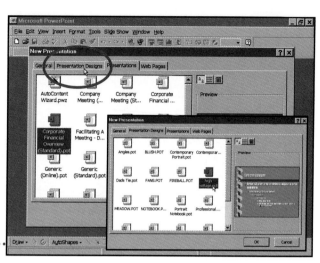

4 You can browse through the generic presentation designs to see what they're like. Click the **Presentation Designs** tab.

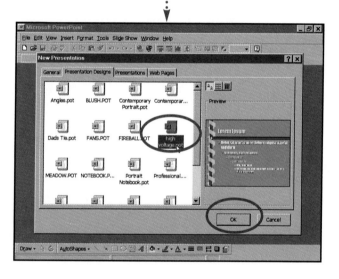

5 Click an icon. A preview of that design appears on the right. Click **OK** to choose it. ■

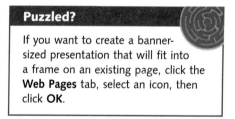

Puzzled?

If you want to create a banner-sized presentation that will fit into a frame on an existing page, click the **Web Pages** tab, select an icon, then click **OK**.

Opening an Existing Presentation

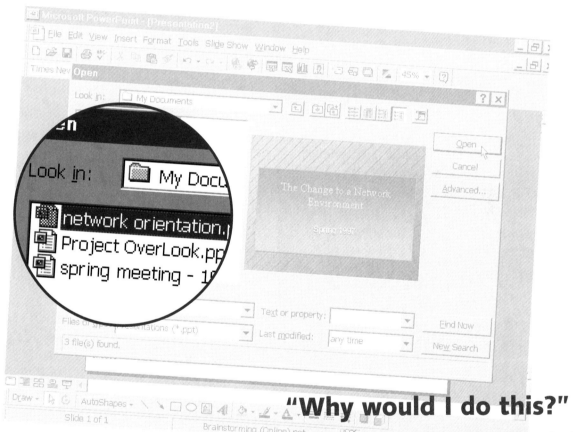

"Why would I do this?"

Most of us have more than one project to work on at a time. Because you save your files on your computer's hard disk or on a floppy disk, you can open an existing presentation file so you can work on it again.

Task 14: Opening an Existing Presentation

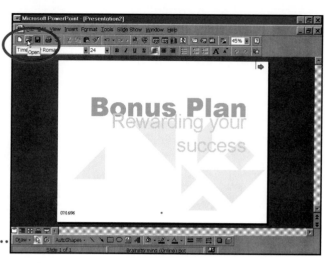

1 Click the **Open** button on the Standard toolbar. The **File** Open dialog box appears.

Missing Link

PowerPoint lists the three most recently used files at the bottom of the File menu. To open a file you've used recently, click on **File** and choose the file's name from the list at the bottom of the menu.

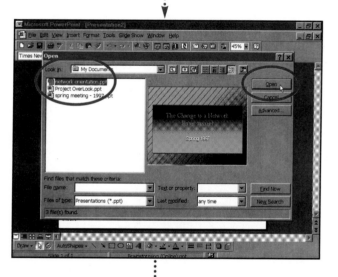

2 Choose the name of the file you want to open. A preview of the selected file appears so you can see if it's the right file. When you're sure, click **Open**.

Puzzled?

If the file you want to open is not listed in the current folder, click the **Look in** drop-down arrow and select the folder in which you saved the file. Then select the file name you want and click **Open**. If you saved a presentation to the Favorites folder, you can locate it by clicking the **Look in Favorites** button. To open a file on the Web, click the **Search the Web** button.

3 The presentation you selected appears on-screen. ■

Puzzled?

You can tell how many files you currently have open by clicking the **Window** menu and looking at the list of open files. The *active* file has a check mark next to its name. If a file is open but you can't see it, open the **Window** menu and click the name of the file you want to see.

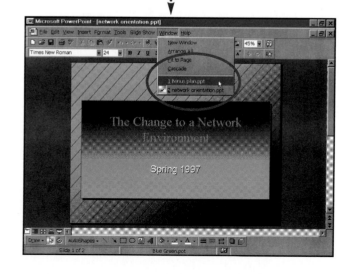

Using the Office Assistant to Get Help

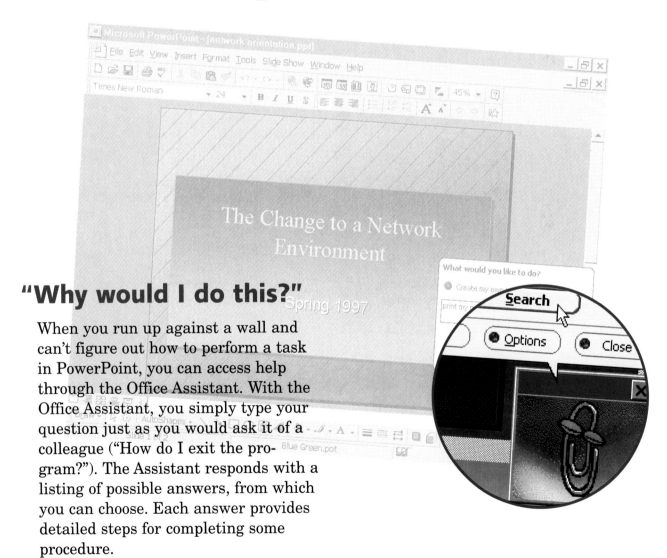

"Why would I do this?"

When you run up against a wall and can't figure out how to perform a task in PowerPoint, you can access help through the Office Assistant. With the Office Assistant, you simply type your question just as you would ask it of a colleague ("How do I exit the program?"). The Assistant responds with a listing of possible answers, from which you can choose. Each answer provides detailed steps for completing some procedure.

1 When you first start PowerPoint, the Office Assistant appears, offering its help. To display the Assistant at a later time, click the **Office Assistant** button on the Standard toolbar.

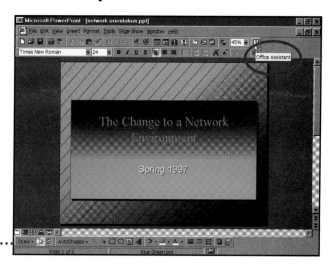

Missing Link

You can also access the Office Assistant by pressing the **F1** key anytime you're working in PowerPoint.

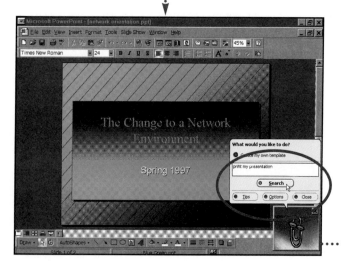

2 The Office Assistant enables you to get information using a question format. Type your question in the text box, and then click **Search**.

3 A list of available topics related to your question appears. Click the topic which best suits your needs. To see additional topics, click **See more**. If you click See more, to return to the previous listing, click **See previous**.

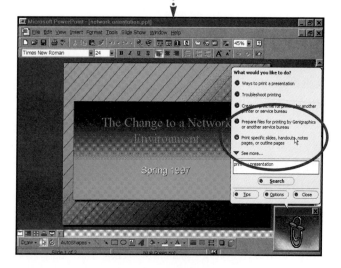

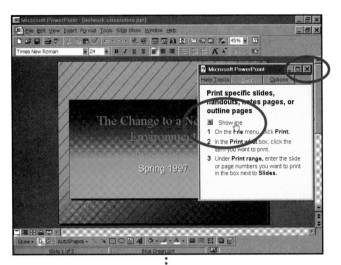

4 A listing of steps describing how to complete that procedure appears. Follow the steps on-screen, then click the **Close** button (the X) to close the Help window and return to PowerPoint.

Puzzled?

If you click on a topic and then change your mind, click the **Close** button (the X) to close the Help window and start over.

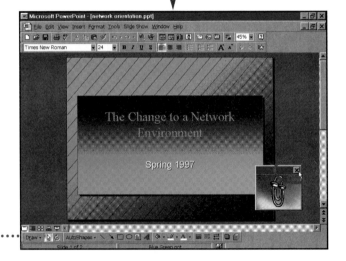

5 The Office Assistant remains on-screen. When you have another question, simply click its title bar, and the text box into which you type your question appears. To remove the Office Assistant from the screen, click its **Close** button (the X).

6 Sometimes, based on your current task, Office Assistant has a suggestion to make. At that time, a small light bulb will appear on the Office Assistant button. To see the suggestion, click the **Office Assistant** button to display the Office Assistant window (if the Office Assistant is already displayed, skip this step).

Task 15: Using the Office Assistant to Get Help

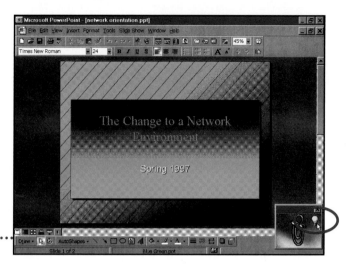

7 In the Office Assistant box, click the light bulb. A suggestion appears.

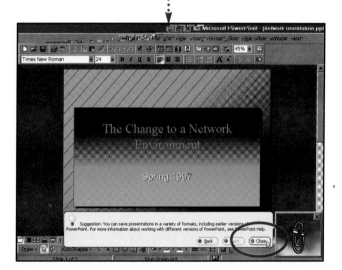

8 Read the suggestion and then click **Close** to remove the suggestion box from the screen. ■

Missing Link

You can click **Back** in the suggestion box to see a previous suggestion. After clicking **Back**, the Next button will no longer appear grayed, which means that you can click it to move forward through the suggestion list.

Exiting Microsoft PowerPoint

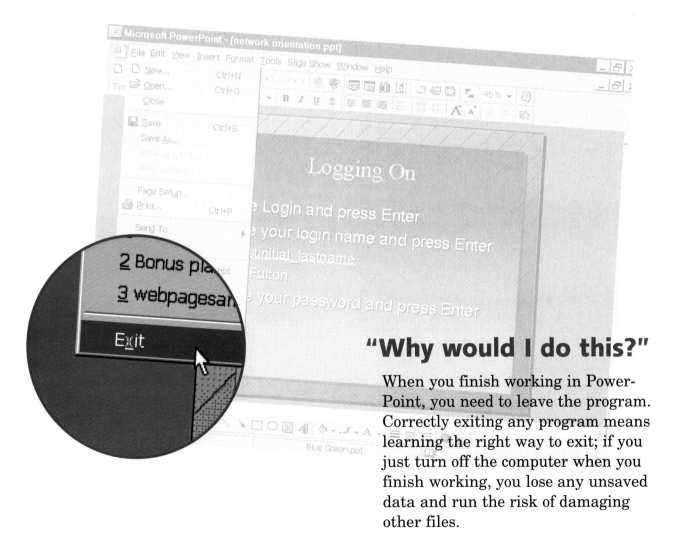

"Why would I do this?"

When you finish working in Power-Point, you need to leave the program. Correctly exiting any program means learning the right way to exit; if you just turn off the computer when you finish working, you lose any unsaved data and run the risk of damaging other files.

Task 16: Exiting Microsoft PowerPoint

1 Open the **File** menu and choose **Exit**. If you haven't made changes to any open files since the last time you saved them, PowerPoint closes the open files and closes down the program. You're returned to the Windows desktop.

Puzzled?

You can also close PowerPoint by clicking on its **Close** button (the X button which appears at the right end of the title bar).

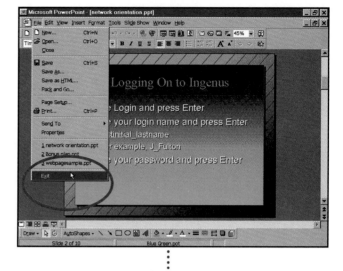

2 If you have open files that contain changes you haven't saved, PowerPoint gives you the opportunity to save them before you exit the program. Choose **Yes** to save your changes. PowerPoint saves the files and then shuts down the program. At that point, you're returned to the Windows desktop.

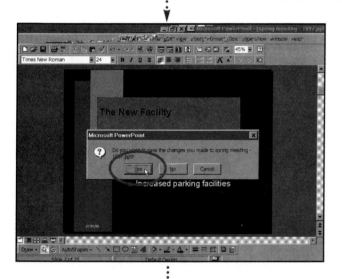

Puzzled?

You can choose **No** to abandon your changes or **Cancel** to return to PowerPoint, and not exit.

3 From the Windows 95 desktop, you can continue working with other programs or shut down your computer. To shut down the computer, click the **Start** button on the taskbar. The Start menu appears. Click **Shut Down**, and you'll see the Shut Down Windows dialog box. Here, click **Shut down the computer?**, and click **Yes**. In a minute or two, you see the message It's now safe to turn off your computer. When you see that message, turn off the computer. ■

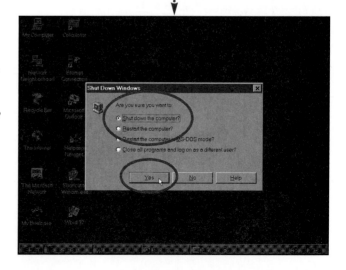

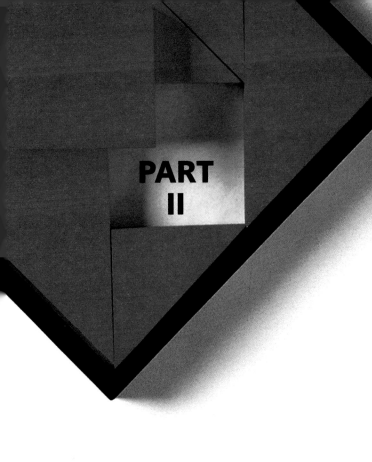

PART II

Working with Text

ONE OF THE MOST IMPORTANT ELEMENTS of any great presentation is its wording. PowerPoint provides many tools you can use to fine-tune and edit your text.

One of the first procedures you'll perform on your text is to edit or change it—because no matter how much time you spend planning your presentation, you're bound to forget something. Fortunately, adding, editing, and deleting text from a slide is easy. You can copy and paste selected text using the Windows Clipboard, and you can delete selected text by pressing the Delete key. In addition, you can move and copy text simply by *dragging* it with your mouse from one spot to another. And because you can cut, copy, and paste information already in your slides, you spend less time typing and more time making your presentation a masterpiece.

One of the most important tools you can use to edit your text is PowerPoint's spell checking utility. Without it, you might ruin an almost perfect presentation with typographical errors. The spell checking utility checks the text in your slides against its built-in dictionary.

In case you forget to use the spelling checker, PowerPoint automatically checks your spelling for commonly misspelled or mistyped words (such as *teh* for *the*) using a feature called AutoCorrect. As you type text on your slides, the AutoCorrect feature compares each word you type with words on the AutoCorrect list to correct the typos you make the most. When it finds a word on the list, it automatically makes the correction—without even telling you! And just as you can with the spell checking utility, you are able to personalize the AutoCorrect list by adding words you often have trouble with.

Not only can you enhance your text with formatting attributes, but you can change the appearance of the text (called the *font*) you use in your slides, as well as the size of the individual characters. Every computer has different fonts installed on it. Common fonts include Times New Roman, Arial, Garamond, and Century Gothic, among others. Fonts come in two basic types: serif and sans serif. A *serif* is an edge found on letters such as s, a, l, and r that makes words easier to distinguish visually; therefore, people commonly use serif fonts in bodies of text. Times New Roman is a serif font. A *sans serif* font has no edges on its characters, which gives it a smoother, cleaner appearance. People often use sans serif fonts for titles, headlines, captions, and other shorter passages of text. Arial is an example of a sans serif font.

After you've adjusted the look of text, you may want to perform other changes. You can choose whether you want text left, right, or center-aligned in titles, for example. You can add bulleted lists instead of using plain text. And you can customize the bullets in a list so they look exactly the way you want them to. A number of symbol fonts (Wingdings, Symbol, and Monotype Sorts, for example) are available for that purpose. Experiment with them to find unique bullet shapes.

In Part II of the book, you learn how to manipulate the slide text by changing its appearance or location.

TASK 17

Editing Existing Text

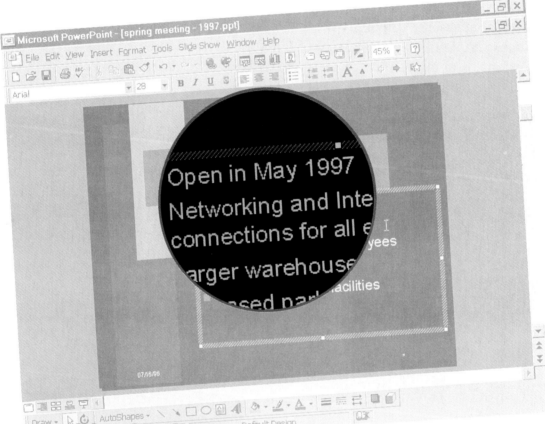

"Why would I do this?"

When you look at your slides, you may find errors in your text, or you may just decide you want to make changes. To edit existing text, you must first activate the box in which it is contained (the text block). When you activate a text block, it is surrounded by a hatched outline. After activating the block, you place the cursor in the spot where you want to edit the text and make changes just as you would in a word processor such as Microsoft Word.

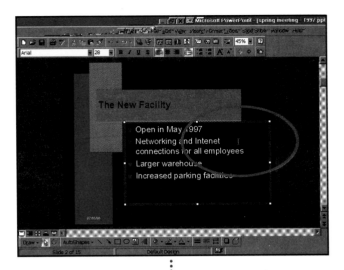

1 Click anywhere within the block that contains the text you want to change. The text block is selected (a hatched outline— an outline with diagonal hatch marks— appears.) The mouse pointer changes to an I-beam. Move the I-beam pointer over the text you wish to change and then click. The *insertion point* (a blinking vertical line) appears in the spot you selected. Press **Delete** to remove characters to the right of the insertion point, press **Backspace** to remove characters to the left, or simply type any text you want to add.

2 After you make your changes, click outside of the selected text block or press the **Esc** key twice. The hatched outline surrounding the text block disappears, and PowerPoint returns you to the slide. ■

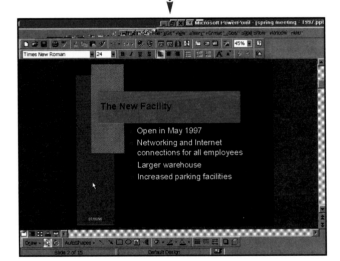

Missing Link

As you make, add, or delete text on a slide, PowerPoint automatically moves your words so they wrap around at the end of each line.

Puzzled?

If you make a change you regret, you can undo it. For example, if you delete a character accidentally, click the **Undo** button on the Standard toolbar, and the character reappears.

Deleting Text

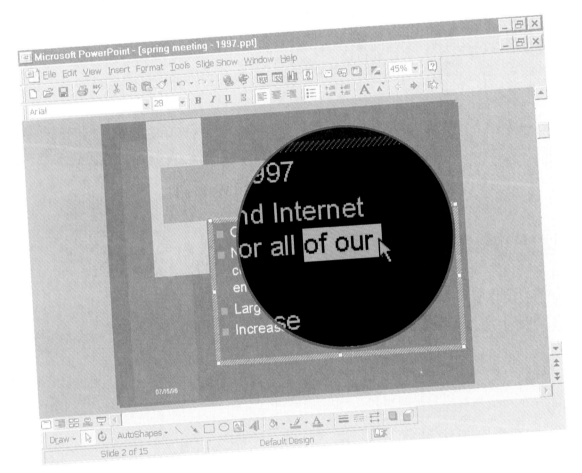

"Why would I do this?"

Not only will you want to change text, but you will also want to delete text from time to time. For example, you might want to delete an entire section of text, or you might want to simply replace it with new words.

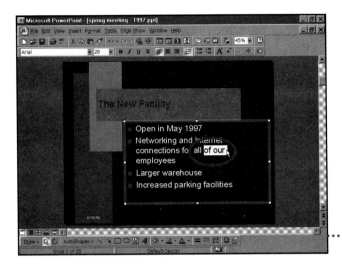

1 Click the block containing the text you want to delete. The text block is highlighted with a hatched outline. Double-click on the word you want to delete to select it. When you select text, its background turns to a different color. You can select a group of words by clicking the mouse button at the beginning of the first word and dragging until all the words you want are highlighted.

2 When you've selected the word(s) you want to delete, press the **Delete** key, or open the **Edit** menu and select **Clear**.

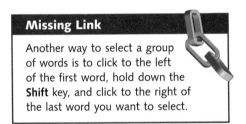

Missing Link

Another way to select a group of words is to click to the left of the first word, hold down the **Shift** key, and click to the right of the last word you want to select.

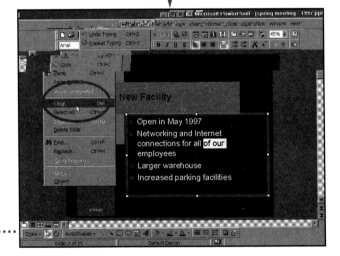

3 The selected words disappear, and PowerPoint rewraps the remaining text to fill in the spot where you deleted the word(s). Click anywhere outside the text block to stop editing, or press **Esc** twice. ■

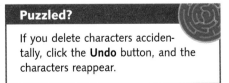

Puzzled?

If you delete characters accidentally, click the **Undo** button, and the characters reappear.

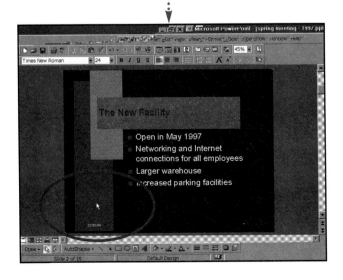

Using Drag and Drop to Copy and Move Text

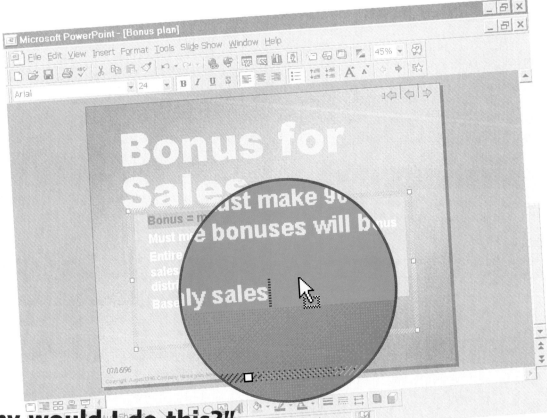

"Why would I do this?"

Suppose you just typed some really nice text, only to realize that it's in the wrong place. Your first impulse might be to delete the text and start typing it again where you want it—but you don't have to do that. PowerPoint has a

handy feature called drag and drop that enables you to use your mouse to move text from one place to another. In addition, you can use drag and drop to quickly copy text.

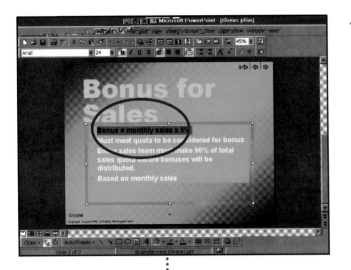

1 Select the appropriate text block by clicking on it. A hashed box appears around the text block. Select the text you want to copy or move by clicking at the beginning of the text section and then dragging to the end of the section you wish to select. PowerPoint highlights the selected text.

Puzzled?

As before, you can also select a group of words by clicking at the beginning of the first word, pressing and holding **Shift**, and clicking at the end of the block you wish to select.

2 Position the mouse pointer over the selected text, press and hold down the left mouse button, and drag the text to move it to its new location. To copy the text instead, press and hold the **Ctrl** key as you drag.

Missing Link

If you're copying text, you'll see a small plus sign under the pointer, in addition to a small square.

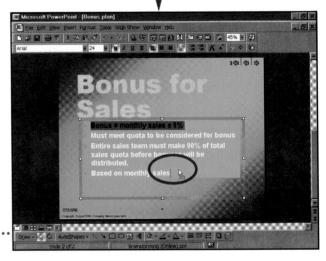

3 When the pointer is in the new location, release the mouse button. PowerPoint "drops" the selected text in the new location. If you're copying text, the original text remains in its place. If you're moving text, the original text is deleted from its location. ■

Puzzled?

If you move or copy text to the wrong location, you can click the **Undo** button, and the text will be restored to its original location.

67

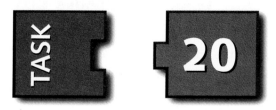

Cutting, Copying, and Pasting Text

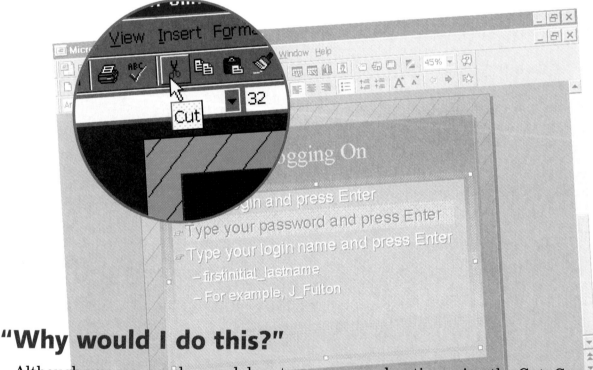

"Why would I do this?"

Although you can use drag and drop to copy or move text on the same slide, you can't use drag and drop to copy or move text from one slide to another. In addition, some people find that it's difficult to control a drag and drop operation, especially if they have trouble using a mouse. You can save yourself a lot of possible frustration by copying or moving existing text and then pasting it in a new location using the Cut, Copy, and Paste commands. When you cut text (in preparation of moving it), PowerPoint removes the text from its original location (see steps 1 and 2) so you can paste it in a new location. When you copy text, PowerPoint leaves the original text intact and makes a copy of it, which you can place in an additional location (see steps 3–5).

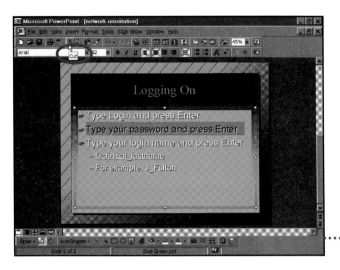

1 Select the text you want to move and click the **Cut** button. PowerPoint places the selected text on the Clipboard and removes it from its original location.

Puzzled?

If you select the wrong text, simply try to select what you want again, or click anywhere on the slide to deselect selected text.

2 Click at the location where you want to place the cut text.

Missing Link

To move (or copy) text to a different slide, simply cut the text and then change to the slide you want by clicking the **Next Slide** or **Previous Slide** buttons on the Vertical scroll bar. Click on that slide at the point where you want the text moved (or copied), then click **Paste**.

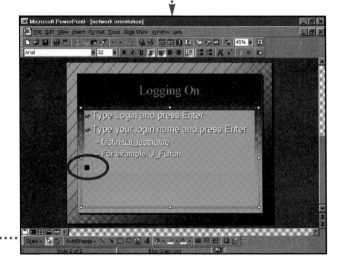

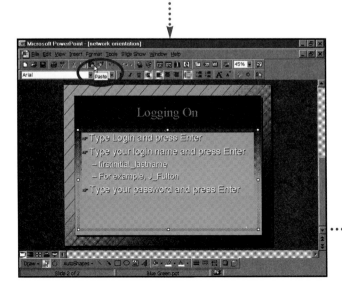

3 Click the **Paste** button. PowerPoint inserts the text from the Clipboard at the location where you clicked.

4 To copy text, select the text you want to copy and click the **Copy** button. The original text stays where it is, and PowerPoint places a copy of it in the Clipboard.

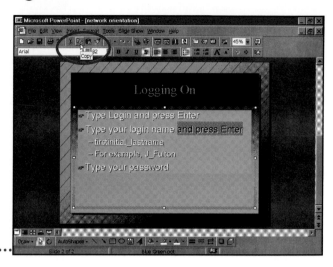

> **Puzzled?**
>
> You can use the contents of the Clipboard more than once without having to recopy the information. Just click the **Paste** button to paste the same text as many times as you need to.

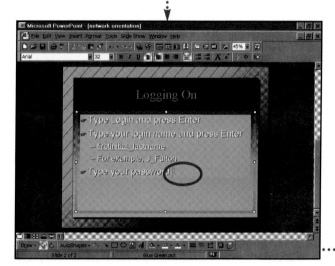

5 Click where you want to place the copied text.

6 Click the **Paste** button. PowerPoint inserts the contents of the Clipboard at the indicated location. ■

> **Missing Link**
>
> The Clipboard is a temporary storage area. The Clipboard holds a copy of the last block of text you cut or copied. If you cut one block of text and then cut another, the second block of text overwrites the first block on the Clipboard.

Adding Bulleted Text

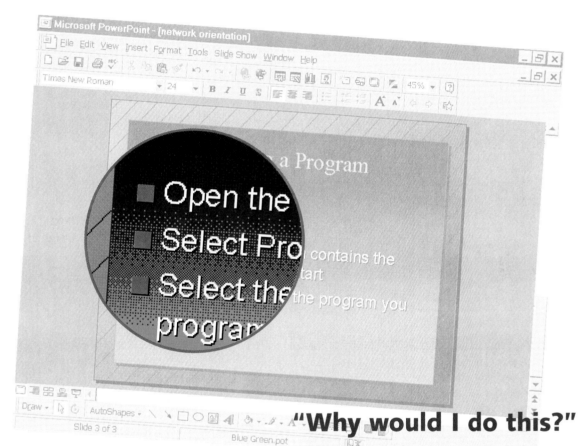

"Why would I do this?"

Many times during a presentation, you will want to summarize what you are trying to say. A bulleted list is ideal for listing these summary points. A *bulleted list* is simply a list of items, each one of which is preceded by a bullet, or small icon—typically a dot. As you'll learn later, you can change this dot to something else, such as a star, a happy face, or a hand.

Task 21: Adding Bulleted Text

1 The layout of a slide determines the elements it contains. If your slide does not contain a bulleted list, then you need to change to a layout which does. To do that, click on the **Slide Layout** button. The Slide Layout dialog box appears.

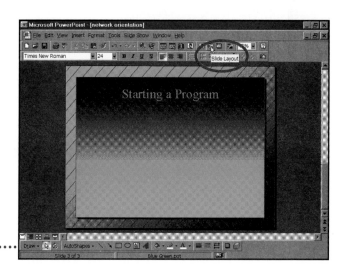

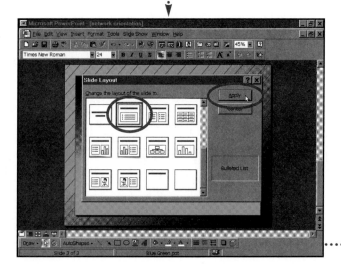

2 Click on a layout design which contains a bulleted list. The layout is highlighted (surrounded by a blue outline). Click **Apply**. The layout of your slide changes to the one you selected.

3 To add your bulleted list, click in the bulleted list box.

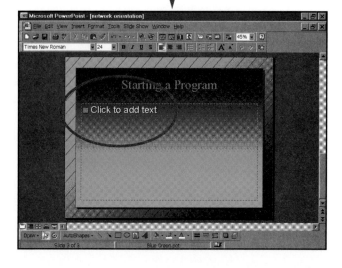

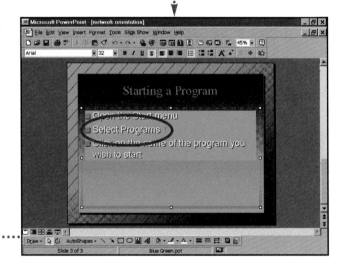

4 Type the first item, and press **Enter**. The cursor moves to the next line and a new bullet appears. Continue adding items as needed, pressing **Enter** after each one.

> **Puzzled?**
>
> When you type the last bulleted item, do not press Enter, or you'll add a blank line with a bullet. If you do press Enter accidentally, press the **Backspace** key.

5 If you need to insert an item in the list, click at the end of the item *above* where you wish to insert your new item. Then press **Enter**. For example, click at the end of item 2 and press **Enter**.

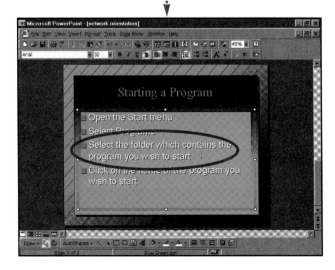

6 A new line appears after item 2. Type your new item on the inserted line. ■

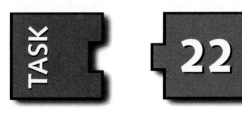

Modifying a Bullet Symbol

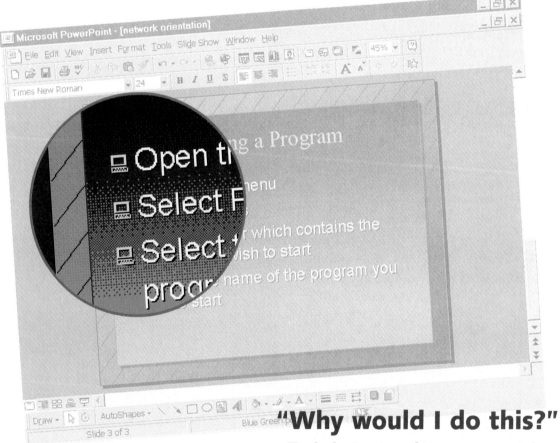

"Why would I do this?"

Each design template uses a certain bullet symbol in front of bulleted text. However, you might want to change the bullet symbol in order to call attention to the bulleted items or to make the symbol fit the theme of your presentation. Changing the bullet symbol is easy and fun.

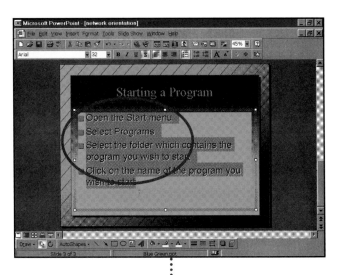

1 Select the lines of text for which you want to change the bullet symbol. The bulleted items you selected are highlighted. (To quickly select all your bulleted items, click inside the bulleted list box and press **Ctrl+A**, or choose **Edit**, **Select All**.)

> **Missing Link**
>
> Try to use no more than two different bullet symbols on any one slide; more than two symbols will detract from the slide's appearance and distract your viewer.

2 Open the **Format** menu and choose **Bullet**. The Bullet dialog box appears.

3 Click on the symbol you want to use for a bullet. Click **OK** and PowerPoint changes the selected bullets to the symbol you selected. If you want, you can change to a different symbol font by selecting it from the **Bullets from** list. (Symbols, like fonts, are installed on an individual basis. If your symbols are different than the ones shown here, you just have different symbols installed.)

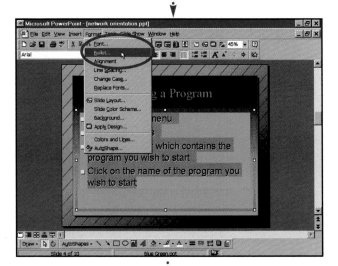

4 If you want to change the size of the bullet *in relation to* the text it's in front of, use the up and down arrows of the **Size** text box. You can change the color of the bullet by clicking the **Color** drop-down arrow and selecting a color from the list. If you want to view more color selections, click **More Colors**.

5 In the Colors dialog box, click a color you like and then click **OK**. ■

TASK

23

Checking Spelling

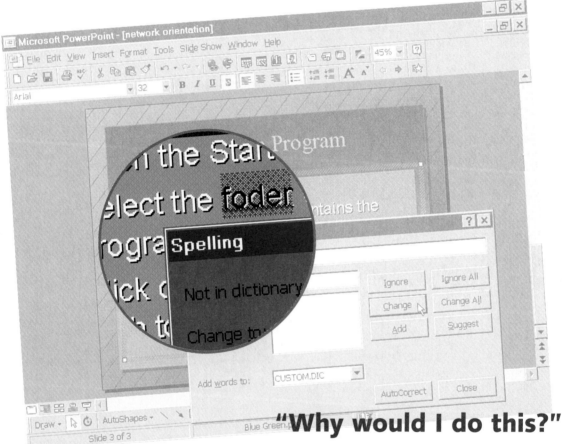

"Why would I do this?"

Everyone makes typographical and spelling errors at one time or another. But it would be a shame to let these errors ruin a beautiful presentation. Fortunately, PowerPoint's spell checking utility and built-in dictionary make it easy to find and fix your spelling errors. PowerPoint even enables you to add your own words to its built-in dictionary.

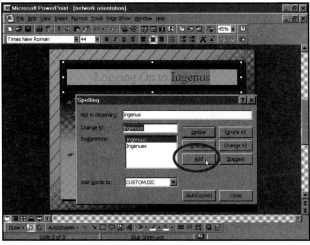

1 Words that PowerPoint feels are misspelled are displayed with a curly red line underneath them. Click the **Spelling** button to start the spell checking utility to correct these error by comparing words in your presentation to words in the Spelling dictionary.

2 When the spell checking utility finds a word that is not in its dictionary, it displays the misspelled word and other suggested spellings. Select a suggestion from the list or type a correction in the **Change to** box. Click **Change** to change the word to the selected suggestion.

3 Even if you spell a word correctly, if it is not in PowerPoint's dictionary, the spelling checker flags it. If you use the word frequently (your company name, for example), click the **Add** button to add it to the dictionary so the spell checking utility will not flag it as a misspelled word.

Puzzled?

If you need to stop the spelling utility before it finishes, click the Close button.

4 When the spell checking utility is through, you'll see a message telling you so. Click **OK** to return to your presentation. ■

Missing Link

You can check the spelling of a single word or a group of words by selecting the text you want to check *before* you click the **Spelling** button. If you don't select any text, the spell checking utility checks the entire presentation—every slide.

Using AutoCorrect

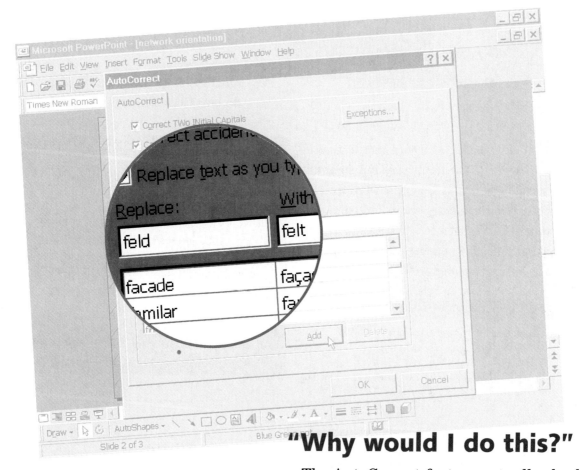

"Why would I do this?"

The AutoCorrect feature actually checks your words as you type and corrects them without even telling you. You can add your own words to AutoCorrect or delete words already in the list. Use this feature to correct words you misspell often, or be creative and use AutoCorrect as your own private "shorthand."

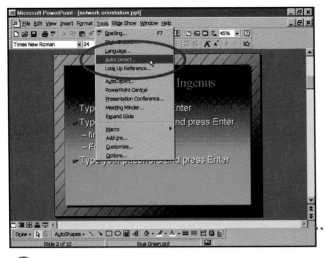

1 Open the **Tools** menu and choose **AutoCorrect**. The AutoCorrect dialog box appears.

2 In the **Replace** text box, type the word as you often misspell it. In the **With** text box, type the word with which you want to replace the misspelled word. Click **Add** to include this entry in the AutoCorrect list. Add as many entries to the list as you want, and then click **OK**.

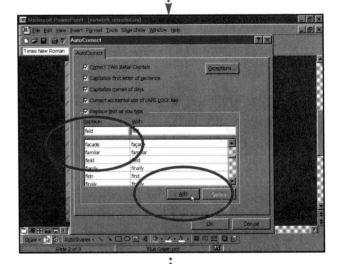

> **Missing Link**
>
> Use AutoCorrect to store "shorthand" for words that require a lot of typing. For example, you can add your initials to the AutoCorrect list and tell AutoCorrect to replace them with your name automatically.

3 To delete an entry from the AutoCorrect list, select it, then click **Delete** to delete the entry. Click **OK** when you finish modifying the AutoCorrect list.

> **Puzzled?**
>
> Using AutoCorrect can affect your computer's performance, particularly if you have an older computer with limited memory. To turn off AutoCorrect, click in the **Replace text as you type** check box to remove the check mark. Then click **OK**.

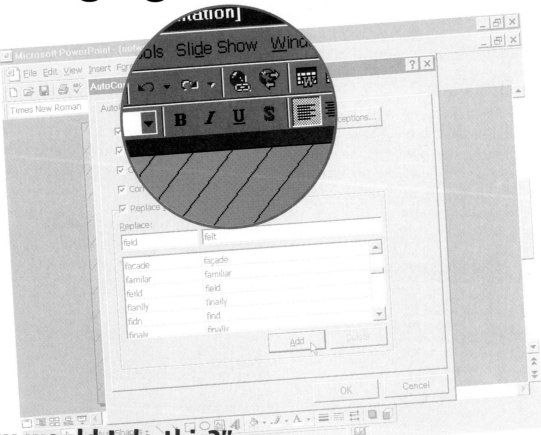

Changing How Text Looks

"Why would I do this?"

As you're perfecting the text in your slides, you might decide you want to emphasize some of the words. You can emphasize text by adding attributes such as boldface, italics, underlining, shadow, or color. You can also add embossing, which makes the text appear as if it has been raised off the slide in a kind of relief. You can easily add bold, italics, underlining, and shadow using buttons on the Formatting toolbar. You can change text color just as easily with the Font Color button on the Drawing toolbar. However, to add embossing, you must use the Font dialog box.

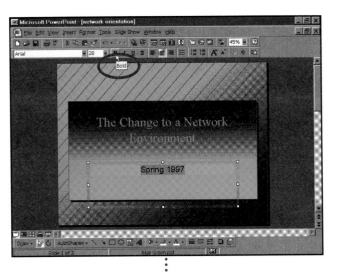

1 Select the word or words you want to make bold and click the **Bold** button on the Formatting toolbar. The selected text appears bold.

Missing Link

When you select a word or character to which one of these attributes has already been applied, the toolbar button appears to be pushed in.

2 Select the word or words you want to italicize and click the **Italic** button instead. The text appears in italics.

Puzzled?

You can combine attributes as you wish by clicking more than one button. For example, you can make a word bold and italic by clicking both the **Bold** and the **Italic** buttons.

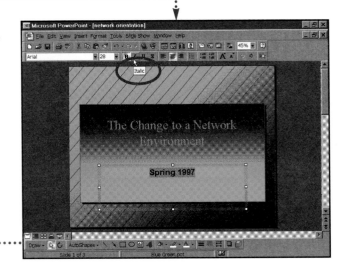

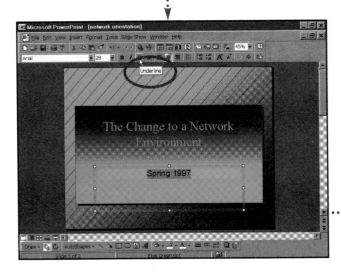

3 Select the text you want to underline and click the **Underline** button. A line appears under the word.

4 Select the text you want to shadow and click the **Shadow** button. The text appears to have a small shadow, falling to the right.

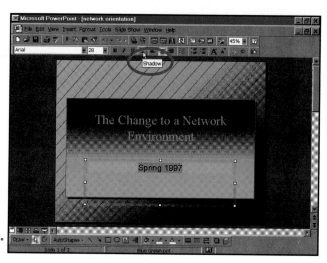

Missing Link

Attribute buttons like the Bold, Italic, Underline, and Shadow are called *toggles*. You click a toggle once to turn the attribute on; you click it again to turn the attribute off. So if you apply an attribute and then change your mind about it, click the toggle button again to turn it off.

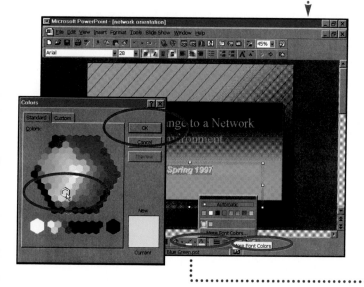

5 Select the text whose color you wish to change, and then click on the **Font Color** down arrow on the Drawing toolbar. Click the color you want. To view additional colors, click on **More Font Colors**. The Colors dialog box appears.

6 Click on a color to select it, and then click **OK**. The selected text changes to the color you selected.

Missing Link

You can add multiple attributes at once by selecting them in the Font dialog box.

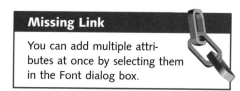

7 To add embossing (a raised relief effect), you must open the Font dialog box. Select the text you wish to change and then open the **Format** menu and select **Font**. The Font dialog box appears.

8 Click on the **Emboss** check box. A check mark appears to tell you that the option is selected. Click **OK**, and embossing is added to the selected text. If you'd like to look at the selected text, click **Preview**. ■

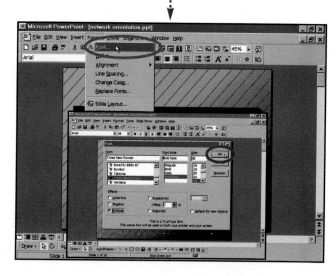

Changing Fonts and Font Sizes

"Why would I do this?"

You might change a font or font size to add emphasis to your text or to create a tone (such as professional or silly) for your document. A *font* is a family of characters that share a similar style and design. Characters within fonts are measured in *points*, and there are 72 points in an inch. The higher the point size, the bigger the character is. You change fonts and font sizes using the Formatting toolbar.

Task 26: Changing Fonts and Font Sizes

1 When you select text, its current font appears in the Font list on the Formatting toolbar. To change a text's font, select the text and then click the **Font** drop-down arrow. Click the font you want. The text changes to the new font, and the font name appears in the Font list on the Formatting toolbar.

> **Puzzled?**
>
> Most computers have certain fonts already installed. As you install new programs, you will add more fonts to your system. Your list might look different from the one in this book.

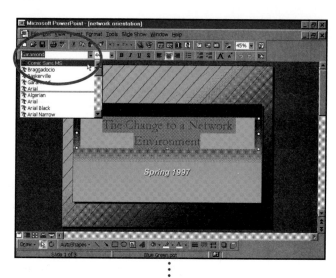

2 You can change the font size of text by selecting it, clicking the **Font Size** drop-down arrow, and clicking the size you want.

> **Missing Link**
>
> Font sizes appear to vary from font to font. For example, 12-point Times New Roman doesn't appear to be the same size as some other 12-point fonts. If you measure the height of the characters, however, the actual point size of the fonts is the same. Because some typefaces spread out more than others, some fonts appear to be larger or smaller.

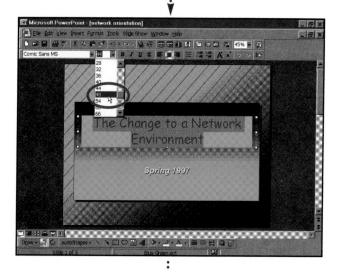

3 You can increase the point size of selected text in increments by clicking the **Increase Font Size** button. To decrease the size of text, click on the **Decrease Font Size button (just to the right of the Increase Font Size button)** instead. You can click on either of these two buttons until the text is the size you want. Using the Increase or Decrease Font Size buttons enables you to determine the size you want by making a visual judgment. ■

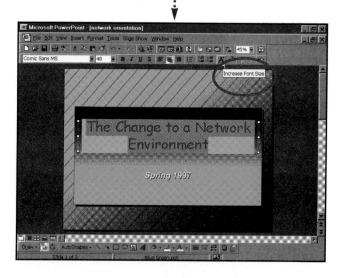

Aligning Text

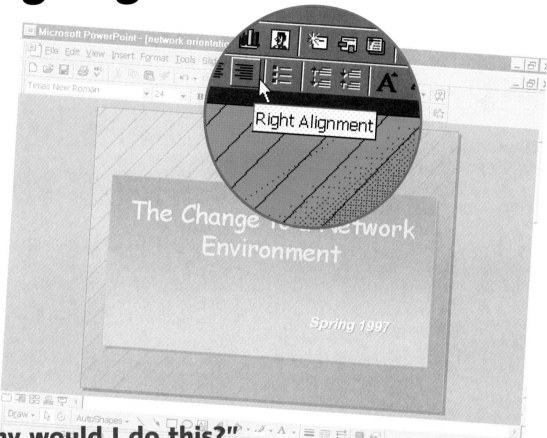

"Why would I do this?"

Part of perfecting your presentation
includes making sure you line up all
your text exactly the way you want it.
For example, you can use text alignment to draw your audience's attention
to a particular part of a slide. You can
align text at the left margin, at the
right margin, or centered between the
left and right margins.

Task 27: Aligning Text

1 To center text, select the text you want to center and click the **Center Alignment** button on the Formatting toolbar. Power-Point centers the text between the margins of the text block.

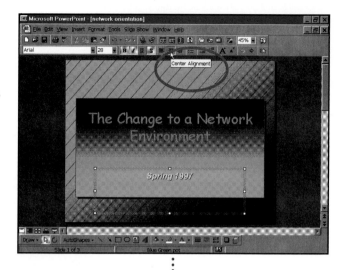

> ### Missing Link
>
> You can justify text (a process which adds spaces between words in order to get the text in a paragraph to touch both the left and right margins) by opening the **Format** menu, selecting **Alignment**, then selecting **Justify**.

2 To align the selected text with the left margin, click the **Left Alignment** button on the Formatting toolbar. PowerPoint aligns all the text at the left margin.

3 To change the alignment of the selected text and make it flush with the right margin, click the **Right Alignment** button on the Formatting toolbar. PowerPoint aligns all the text at the right margin. ■

> ### Puzzled?
>
> When you use the Alignment buttons, text is aligned *within its text block*. You can reposition the text block on the slide by clicking it. A hashed border appears. Hold down the mouse button, and drag the block to its new location. Release the mouse button, and the text block is moved to that point.

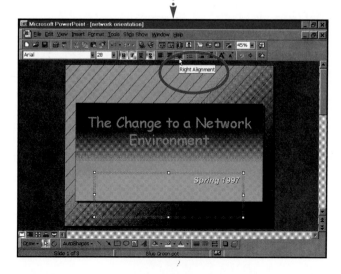

Using WordArt to Enhance Text

"Why would I do this?"

Have you ever seen text that looks like it has been stretched or bent around a curve? You can create these same effects in your slides with a feature called

WordArt. WordArt offers many patterns with which you can shape your text. In addition, you can make modifications to your WordArt shape as needed.

Task 28: Using WordArt to Enhance Text

1 Click on the **Insert WordArt** button, located on the Drawing toolbar. The WordArt Gallery dialog box appears.

2 Select a style that you like, and it's highlighted with a dark border. You'll be able to modify this style later on, as needed. Click **OK**, and the Edit WordArt Text dialog box appears.

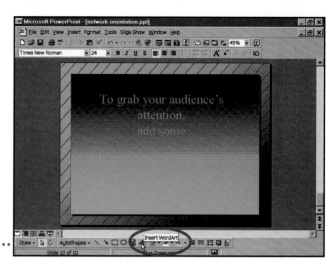

3 Enter your text. You can change its font and its size by making selections from the **Font** and **Size** lists. In addition, you can add bold or italics attributes by clicking on their buttons. Your text will change based on your selections. When you're through, click **OK**. After a few moments, your WordArt text appears in the center of the slide.

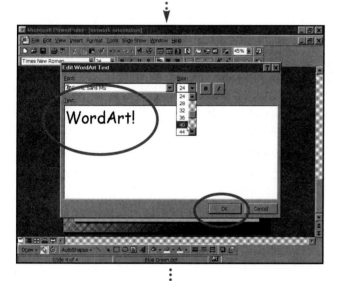

> **Puzzled?**
>
> You don't have to select the text in the WordArt Gallery dialog box in order to change its font, size, or attributes.

4 When the WordArt object is selected, it's surrounded by tiny boxes called *handles*. To move the object, move the mouse pointer over the text (it will change to a four-headed arrow). Click and hold the mouse button down as you drag the WordArt object to its new location. You'll see an outline of the WordArt object as you drag. Release the mouse button, and the WordArt object is moved to its new location.

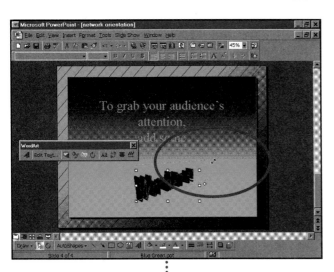

5 You can resize the WordArt object by clicking on one of its handles and dragging that handle outward (to make the WordArt bigger) or inward (to make it smaller). As you move the mouse pointer over one of the handles, it changes to a two-headed arrow. As you drag, you see a shadow of the WordArt object, so you can judge the changes you're making to its size. When you release the mouse button, the WordArt object is resized.

6 You make changes to the WordArt object with the WordArt toolbar. For example, if you want to change the shape of the WordArt object, click the **WordArt Shape** button. A listing of various shapes appears. Click on a shape, and your WordArt object is changed to that shape.

Puzzled?

The WordArt toolbar should appear automatically whenever you click on the WordArt object to select it. However, if for some reason, you don't see the WordArt toolbar, you can make it appear by opening the **View** menu, selecting **Toolbars**, and then clicking **WordArt**.

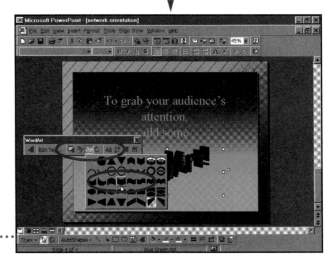

7 To change the color of your WordArt object, click the **Format Word Art** button on the WordArt toolbar. The Format WordArt dialog box appears.

8 Click on the **Colors and Lines** tab. To change the color of your WordArt text, click the **Color** list and click on a color. After making your selection, click **OK**, and your WordArt object is changed to the color you selected.

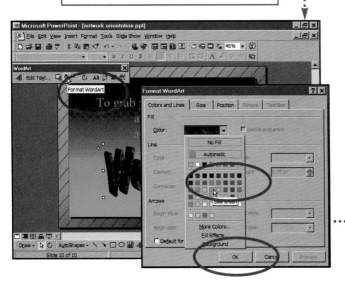

9 To view more colors, click **More Colors** from the **Color** list. The Colors dialog box appears. Click on a color, and your selection appears in the New box, while the old color appears in the Current box. Click **OK** to return to the Format WordArt dialog box.

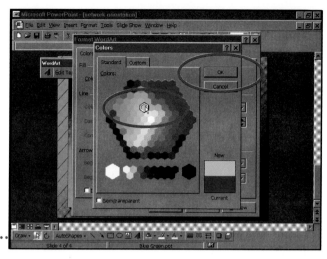

10 To add texture to your WordArt text, select **Fill Effects** from the **Color** list instead. You can select from a gradient, textured, pattern, or picture fill. Click the appropriate tab, click on a selection, and click **OK**. For example, click the Texture tab, click on White Marble (your selection appears in the Sample box), and click **OK**.

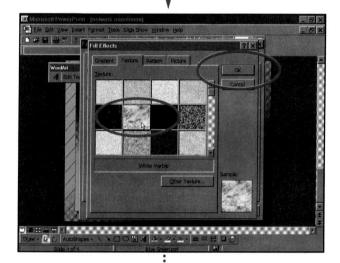

> **Puzzled?**
>
> If you don't like your WordArt object and you want to start over, click it to select it and then press **Delete**.

11 With the other buttons on the WordArt toolbar, you can select a different shape from the WordArt gallery, edit the Word-Art text, rotate the WordArt object, change the text letters to the same height, position the text so it reads vertically rather than horizontally, change the alignment of the text within the text box, and change the spacing between text characters. ■

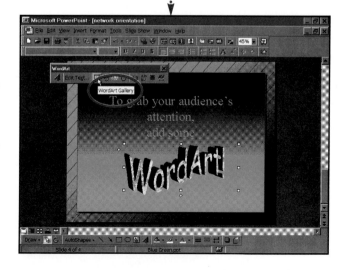

PART III

Adding Clip Art to Your Slides

AFTER YOU WRITE AND PERFECT THE TEXT for your presentation, it's time to have some fun jazzing up your slides with artwork. With PowerPoint, you can place *clip art* (electronic files of pre-designed art) directly on your slides.

Of course, clip art can add more than just entertainment value to your slides: It can reinforce your text, show a product, or create a mood for your presentation. Careful use of artwork and color can even "set the tone" of your presentation. For example, if you insert a humorous cartoon instead of a serious picture, it lets your audience know you want them to laugh, relax, and enjoy the presentation. Of course, you probably don't want every piece of artwork to be funny, but one or two pieces of humorous clip art can put the audience at ease.

Microsoft PowerPoint comes with hundreds of clip art pictures that you can easily insert on any slide. The Microsoft ClipArt Gallery organizes this clip art into categories for you. The Gallery is easy to use. To find artwork you want, simply open the ClipArt Gallery, select a category you like, and then choose from the miniature samples (called *thumbnails*) of the images in each category. Like a real art gallery, the ClipArt Gallery displays the contents of each category so you can view them at a glance. You then select the image you want to use, and if you don't want to wade through the Microsoft ClipArt Gallery to select an image for every slide, AutoClipArt can select several for you, based on the contents of the presentation.

You can insert as many pieces of clip art on a slide as you want (although using more than a few may detract from the slide's text). Once you insert a piece of clip art, you can move it around on the slide or make it larger or smaller—whatever it takes to make it look "just right." You select clip art just as you do text. However, when you select a clip art image, tiny rectangles called *handles* appear around it. These handles enable you to move and resize the image. In addition, you can exclude areas of the image (a process which is called *cropping*), and you can cut, copy, paste, and delete clip art using techniques similar to those you use when working with text.

And, as if it isn't enough that PowerPoint supplies you with all of this wonderful clip art, PowerPoint also allows you to add any clip art you buy separately or scan on your own (such as a company logo) to the ClipArt Gallery. The ability to add your own clip art makes the ClipArt Gallery a virtual "one-stop shopping" area for presentation artwork.

Even if your words have power and your artwork looks spectacular, sometimes you need to add your own personal touch to the slides by adding an arrow or a cartoon balloon with a comment. PowerPoint includes a wide variety of drawing tools that enable you to accomplish these tasks with ease and achieve professional-looking results. In addition, PowerPoint provides a variety of commonly used shapes (called AutoShapes) that you can add to the slides, which can be moved and resized to your liking. This part of the book shows you how to add and manipulate the artwork on your slides to create professional flair!

TASK 29

Inserting Clip Art

"Why would I do this?"

Artwork makes your slides special. You can add predesigned artwork called *clip art* to your slides to get people's attention, change their moods, or add emphasis to your spoken words. Artwork always dresses up plain-looking slides.

You've heard the expression "a picture is worth a thousand words"? Well, it's true!

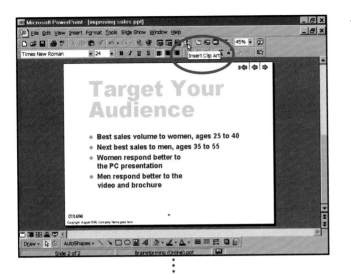

1 With the slide to which you want to add clip art displayed on-screen in Slide view, click the **Insert Clip Art** button on the Standard toolbar. You may see a message telling you that you can install additional clip art images from the PowerPoint CD. Click **OK** to add the images to the ClipArt Gallery

Puzzled?

Many types of electronic art-work are available in file formats that are compatible with PowerPoint.

2 If needed, click the **Clip Art** tab. Scroll through the available categories in the **Categories** list, and click on one. The pic-tures in the selected category appear in the pictures box. Scroll through the pictures until you find one you want. Click on the desired clip art and click the **Insert** button.

Puzzled?

Your Microsoft ClipArt Gallery might contain different images from those shown in this book. Because you can add other files to the Gallery, your computer might have more or less clip art installed on it.

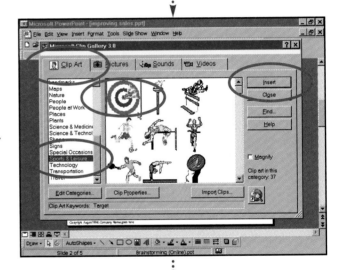

3 The clip art appears on your slide. Black or white squares called *handles* surround the image, indicating that it is selected. The Picture toolbar also appears. Press the **Esc** key to deselect the image. ■

Missing Link

When adding clip art to your slides. You can insert clip art that came with any other program installed on your computer, using the **Insert**, **Picture**, **From File** command.

97

Using AutoClipArt

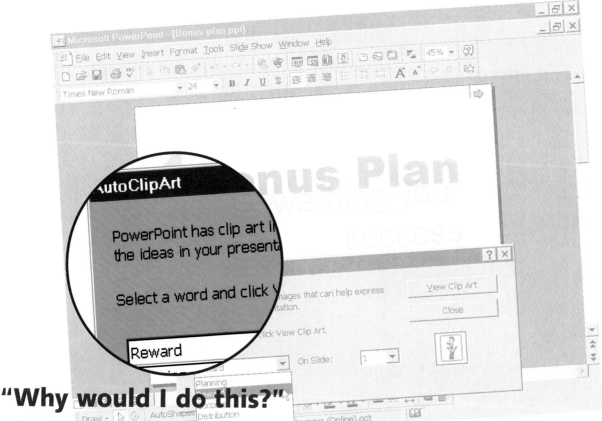

"Why would I do this?"

AutoClipArt is a feature which suggests clip art images for the slides in your presentation, based on the content of the slides. After reviewing your words, AutoClipArt presents you with a selection of clip art images that echo your meaning. Use AutoClipArt to avoid the hassle of reviewing every picture in the Microsoft ClipArt Gallery just to find appropriate pieces of art.

When you start AutoClipArt, it scans the text in your presentation for keywords, such as "target," "spirit," or "winner." It then scans the Microsoft ClipArt Gallery for artwork which match these key words. You browse through these selections and insert the pictures you want to use on the slides on which you want art.

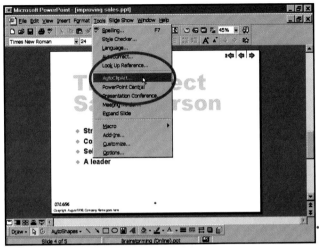

1 Open the **Tools** menu and select **AutoClipArt**. PowerPoint scans your presentation looking for keywords.

2 After AutoClipArt reviews your presentation's text, it displays the AutoClipArt dialog box. Select a key word from the first list. If the keyword appears on several slides, you can select which slide you want to insert the clip art on by selecting the slide number from the second list. The slide appears under the dialog box, so you can see the text to which the keyword refers. Click **View Clip Art**.

Puzzled?

If the text in your presentation doesn't match the keywords for any of the artwork in the Gallery, then you'll see a message telling you so. You can still locate an image on your own, by clicking **View Clip Art**.

3 You may see a message telling you to insert the PowerPoint CD. If you want the additional clips, insert the CD and click **OK**. The Microsoft Clip Gallery 3.0 dialog appears. Scroll through the images that match the keyword you selected. Click an image, then click **Insert** to add it to the slide. After that, you're returned to the AutoClipArt dialog box. Select another keyword if you like, and repeat step 3 to insert an image on the same or a different slide. When you're done, click **Close** to close the AutoClipArt dialog box. ∎

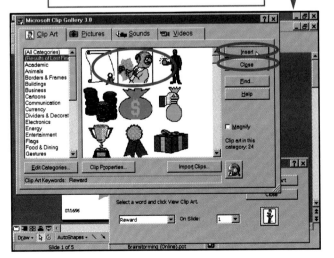

Moving Clip Art

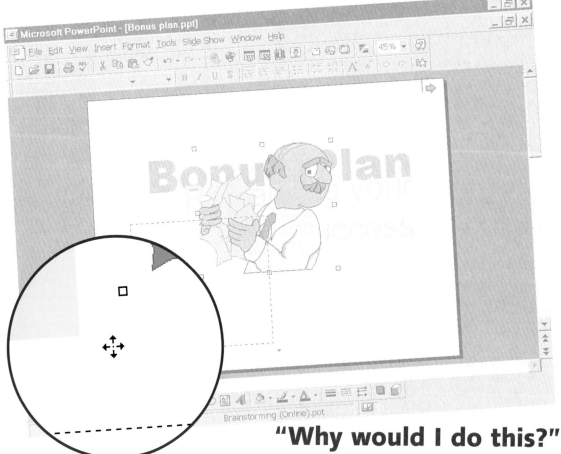

"Why would I do this?"

When you insert clip art on a slide, it appears in the center of that slide, which is rarely the exact spot where you want it. Moving artwork on a slide is as easy as clicking and dragging. By selecting the image and then dragging it, you can place the image exactly where you want it.

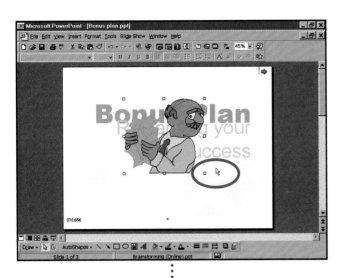

1 When an image is selected, square handles appear all around it. (The Picture toolbar may also appear, if it is not turned off on the View, Toolbars menu.) If the image you want to move isn't selected, click on it once to select it.

Puzzled?

You absolutely cannot move clip art unless you first select the image.

2 Move the mouse pointer over the center of the image. It will change to a pointer and four-headed arrow. Press and hold the mouse button, and drag. As you drag, a dotted outline moves with the drop-and-drag pointer. When the dotted outline seems to be in the place you want the image, release the mouse button.

Puzzled?

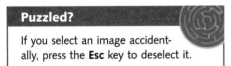

If you select an image accidentally, press the **Esc** key to deselect it.

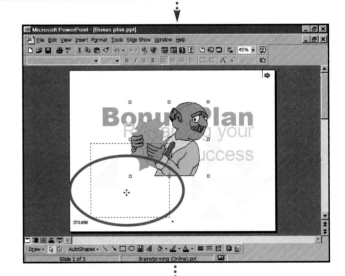

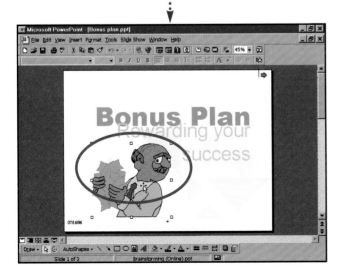

3 The image appears in its new location, still surrounded by handles. If it's not exactly right, click and drag the image as many more times as necessary. When you're satisfied, press the **Esc** key to deselect the image. ■

Missing Link

You can simultaneously move more than one piece of artwork on a slide by holding down the **Shift** key and clicking on each image you want to select. Then you simply drag the group.

Resizing Clip Art

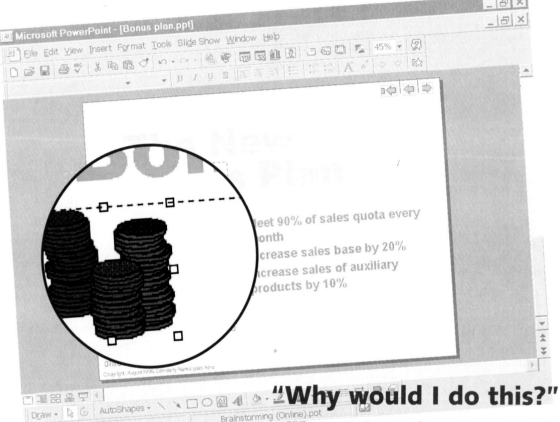

"Why would I do this?"

When you insert clip art in a slide, it probably won't automatically appear in the exact size you want. However, you can easily increase or decrease the size of the image using your mouse. For example, if the clip art you insert is so small that it seems lost on your slide, you can increase the size of the image to fill the space you have available.

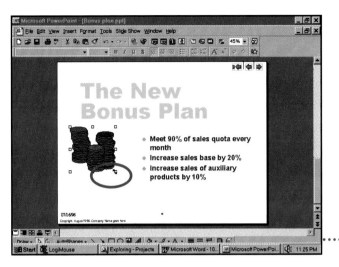

1 If the image you want to move is not already selected, click on it. When selected, handles surround the image (and the Picture toolbar may appear). Once you've selected your image, position the mouse pointer over one of the corner handles. The pointer changes to a double-headed diagonal arrow.

2 Hold down the **Ctrl** key, press and hold the mouse button, and drag the mouse. Although you could resize this coin image without using the Ctrl key, holding down Ctrl forces PowerPoint to maintain the image's proportions.

Puzzled?

If you use the Ctrl key to preserve the image's proportions, the outline might not change as you resize, or it might appear to jump. The outline doesn't change until the proportions are accurate; when the image reaches an acceptable dimension, the outline jumps to a new size.

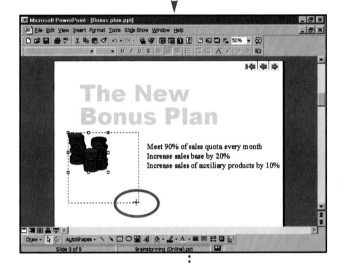

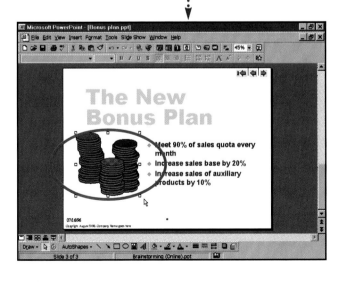

3 When you release the mouse button, PowerPoint displays the image in its new size, surrounded by handles. Press the **Esc** key to deselect the image. ■

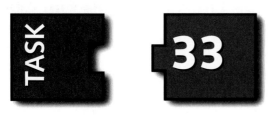

Cropping Clip Art

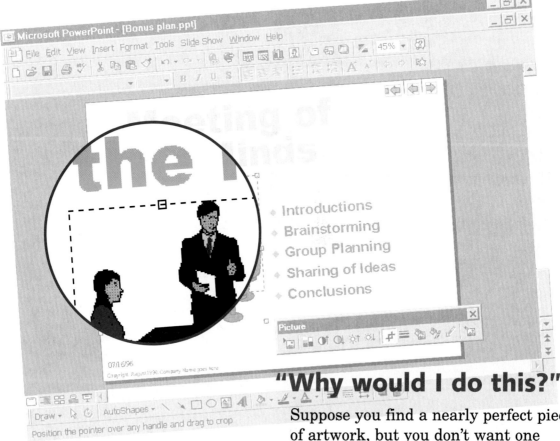

"Why would I do this?"

Suppose you find a nearly perfect piece of artwork, but you don't want one small edge of the image on your slide. You can insert the image into your slide and then crop out the unwanted part. *Cropping* is like placing a piece of white paper over an unwanted area of a photograph. Of course, those areas are still there, they're just not visible. Fortunately, in PowerPoint, that hidden area won't appear at all; it's as if the unwanted part never existed!

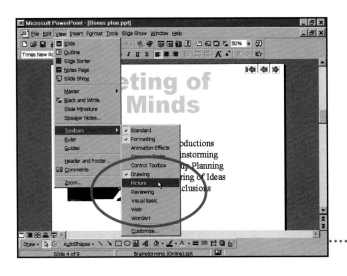

1 Select the image you want to crop by clicking on it. Then (if the Picture toolbar is not visible) open the **View** menu, select **Toolbars**, and select **Picture**. The Picture toolbar appears.

Missing Link

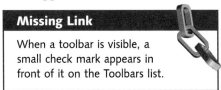

When a toolbar is visible, a small check mark appears in front of it on the Toolbars list.

2 Click the **Crop** tool. Place the cropping tool pointer over the handle on the side, top, or bottom of the image you want to crop.

Puzzled?

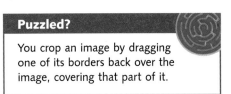

You crop an image by dragging one of its borders back over the image, covering that part of it.

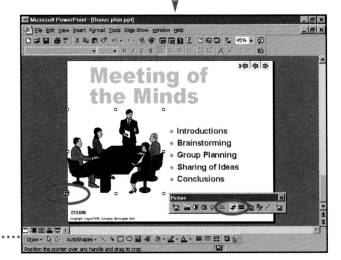

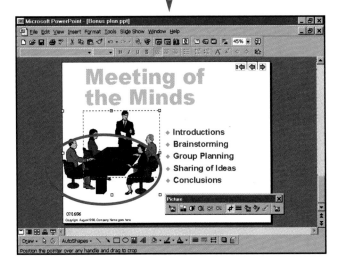

3 Press and hold the mouse button and drag the pointer back over the part of the image you want to hide. You see an outline of the visible image; that outline shows you how much of the image will remain when you release the mouse button. When the material you want to exclude is no longer visible in the outline, release the mouse button. ■

Copying Clip Art

"Why would I do this?"

If you want to use a piece of artwork on more than one slide, you can always go through the process of inserting it again. However, it's usually easier to copy the image to the Clipboard and paste it into another location. Copying can be especially efficient when you need to reproduce an image that you've already resized or cropped.

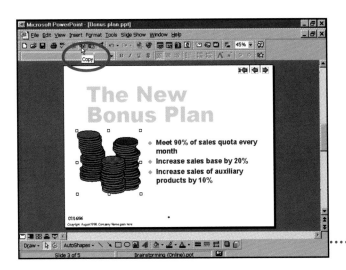

1 Select the image you want to copy by clicking on it. Handles appear to show that the image is selected. (The Picture toolbar may also appear.) Click the **Copy** button on the Standard toolbar.

2 Switch to another slide if necessary. Click the **Paste** button. PowerPoint pastes a copy of your image on the slide. If you're pasting on the same slide, the copy appears on top of the original image. The new image is not directly on top of the original; you can see both images.

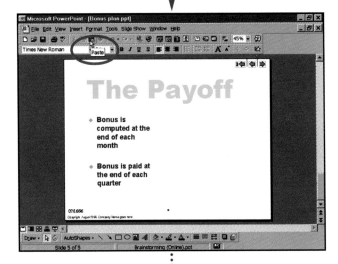

Missing Link

You can move, resize, and crop the pasted image just as you would any other image. For more information on these procedures, see Part 3, Tasks 31, 32, and 33.

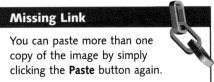

3 To move the image, position the mouse pointer over it, press and hold the mouse button, and drag the pasted image. An outline of the image moves with the drag-and-drop pointer as you drag. When the outline seems to be where you want it, release the mouse button. ■

Missing Link

You can paste more than one copy of the image by simply clicking the **Paste** button again.

Adding the Same Image to Every Slide

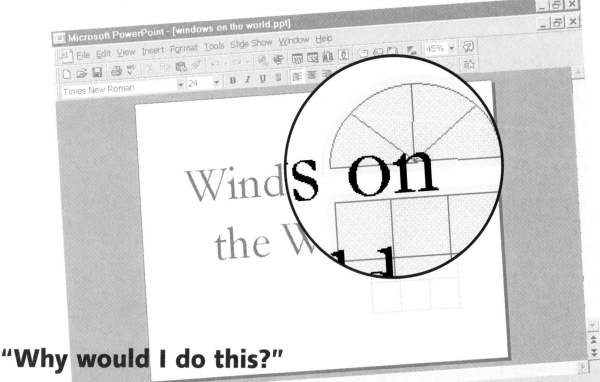

"Why would I do this?"

If you have a special image that ties your presentation together, you may want to add it to the background of every slide. For example, if your presentation is called "Windows on the World," you may want to add a small globe or a window to each slide. This gives your presentation an identity, and helps to remind the audience of your theme.

Of course, you can add other graphics as well, such as a company logo, an image from a recent ad campaign, or a simple design graphic. In any case, to add the graphic to every slide, you add it to the Slide Master. The Slide Master contains the common slide elements, such as margins, text styles, headers, footers, and graphics.

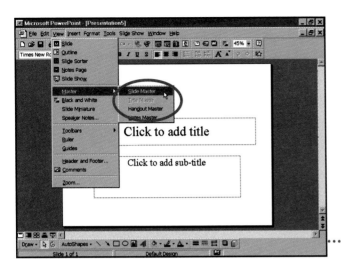

1 Open the **View** menu and select **Master**, then select **Slide Master**. The master slide appears.

2 Click the **Insert Clip Art** button. The Microsoft Clip Gallery 3.0 dialog appears.

3 Select a **Category**, then scroll through the images and click one to select it. Click **Insert** to insert the clip art you selected.

4 The image you selected appears on the master slide. Make adjustments. When you're done, click the **Close** button on the Master toolbar. (If for some reason, the Master toolbar is not visible, use the **View**, **Toolbars** command to display it.) ■

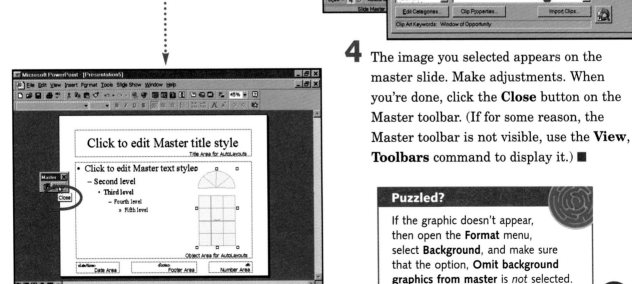

Puzzled?

If the graphic doesn't appear, then open the **Format** menu, select **Background**, and make sure that the option, **Omit background graphics from master** is *not* selected.

Deleting Clip Art

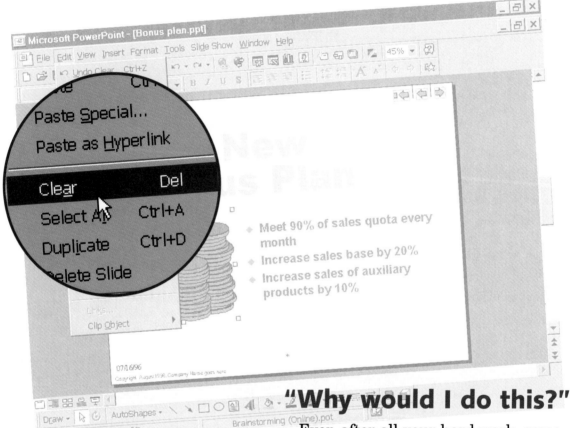

"Why would I do this?"

Even after all your hard work, sometimes a piece of artwork just isn't right, and the only alternative is to delete it. Deleting an image is just like deleting a word: You select the image and click the **Cut** button (to move the image to the Clipboard) or press the **Delete** key.

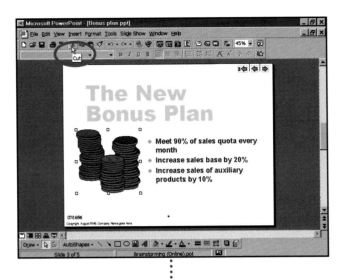

1 Select the image you want to delete and click the **Cut** button on the Standard toolbar. When you use the Cut button, PowerPoint places the image in the Clipboard; you can paste the image somewhere else by clicking on the **Paste** button.

> **Puzzled?**
>
> You can delete the image permanently by selecting it and then pressing **Delete**. When you use the Delete key (or the Edit, Clear command), PowerPoint *does not* place the image in the Clipboard.

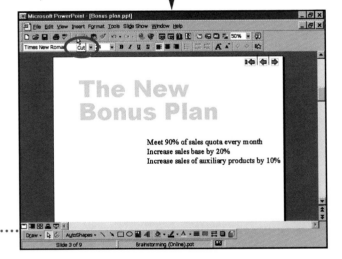

2 The image disappears. If you used the Cut command, you can paste the deleted image to another slide.

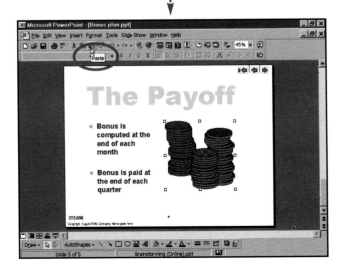

3 You can paste the deleted image on another slide by changing to that slide and clicking the **Paste** button. ■

> **Puzzled?**
>
> If you delete artwork accidentally, click the **Undo** button immediately.

111

Adding Clip Art to the Gallery

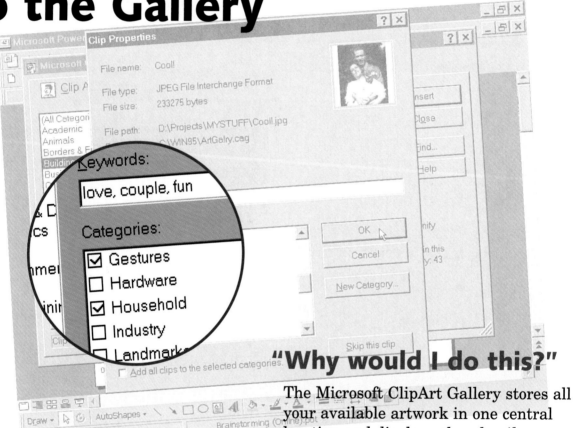

"Why would I do this?"

The Microsoft ClipArt Gallery stores all your available artwork in one central location and displays *thumbnails* (miniature pictures) of each picture so you can see what you're selecting. You can add your own images to the Gallery to take advantage of those features. If you have a logo, a business card, or other artwork stored in an electronic file, you can add that file to the Microsoft ClipArt Gallery for use within PowerPoint and any of your other Microsoft Office programs, such as Microsoft Word.

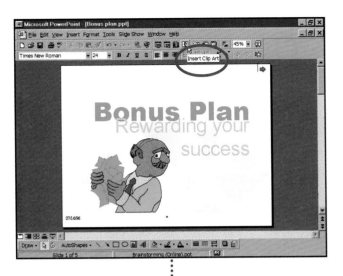

1 Click the **Insert Clip Art** button. The Microsoft Clip Gallery 3.0 dialog box appears. If you want to install additional clip art, insert the CD and click **OK**.

Puzzled?

It doesn't matter what slide is currently displayed when you click the **Insert Clip Art** button.

2 Click the **Import Clips** button in the Microsoft ClipArt Gallery dialog box. PowerPoint displays the Add clip art to Clip Gallery dialog box.

Missing Link

If you don't like the way the ClipArt Gallery organizes graphic images, click the **Edit Categories** button in the Organize ClipArt dialog box to add, rename, or delete categories.

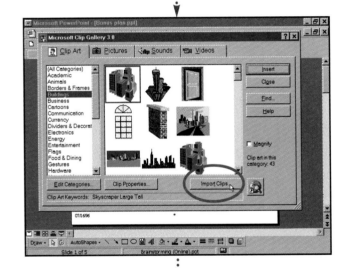

3 Select the files you wish to import, and click the **Open** button.

Puzzled?

To select adjacent files, click the first file, press and hold **Shift**, then click the last file in the group. To select nonadjacent files, press and hold **Ctrl** as you click each file.

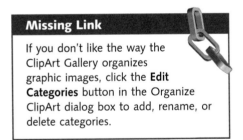

4 A thumbnail of the first selected file appears in the upper right-hand corner of the dialog box. Select the categorie(s) into which you want this clip art placed. A check mark appears in front of the selected categories. Type keywords that describe your clip art in the **Keywords** text box. Separate each keyword with a comma, like this: **victory, proud, winner**. Click **OK**.

Puzzled?

You can create a new one by clicking the **New Category** button, typing a category name, and clicking **OK**.

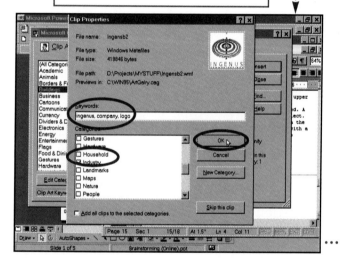

5 Repeat step 4 for each additional file you selected. When you're done adding clip art, you're automatically returned to the Microsoft Clip Gallery 3.0 dialog box.

Missing Link

If you originally selected a file which you've decided not to add to the Clip Gallery, click **Skip this clip**.

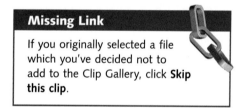

6 Click **Close** to return to PowerPoint. ■

Missing Link

If you have an Internet connection, you can add clip art from the Microsoft Web site. First, connect to the Internet in the usual manner. Then click the **Connect to Web for additional clips button** (the globe), located at the bottom right-hand corner of the Microsoft Clip Gallery 3.0 dialog box.

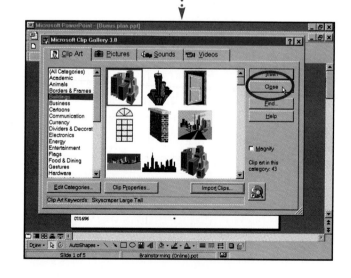

Using Drawing Tools

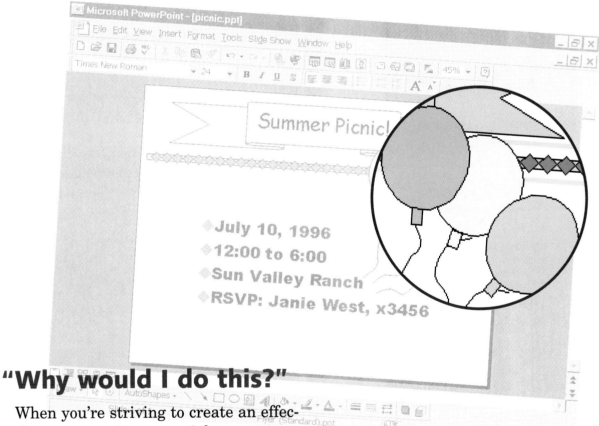

"Why would I do this?"

When you're striving to create an effective presentation, you might want to take advantage of special drawing tools to highlight some special information. For example, you might want to add some stars or a banner; or if you're using a cartoon image, you might want to add a "balloon comment" (like the bubbles that appear above cartoon character's heads). You can help the audience better understand a slide by using one of these methods.

Task 38: Using Drawing Tools

1 Select the slide you want to draw on and click on one of the buttons on the Drawing toolbar. To add a banner, for example, click on the **AutoShapes** button.

Puzzled?

If the Drawing toolbar is not displayed, open the **View** menu, select **Toolbars**, and select **Drawing** to display it.

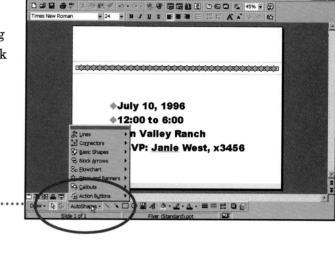

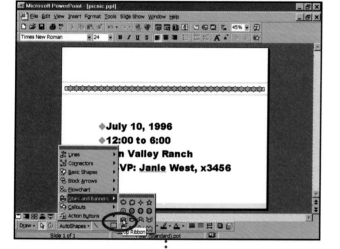

2 Select a category, then click on the shape you want to use. For example, to add the banner, select the **Stars and Banners** category, then click on the banner shape you like.

Puzzled?

The color and style of an object can be changed by simply clicking the object to select it and then clicking the appropriate button on the Drawing toolbar: Fill Color, Line Color, Font Color, Line Style, Dash Style, Arrow Style, Shadow, or 3-D.

3 The mouse pointer changes to a small cross. Click on the slide where you want the upper left-hand corner of the shape to be, then drag downward and to the right to create the shape. Release the mouse button when the shape is the size you want.

Puzzled?

If you don't place the shape in the right spot, you can move it by clicking it and dragging it where you want. You can resize it by dragging one of its handles.

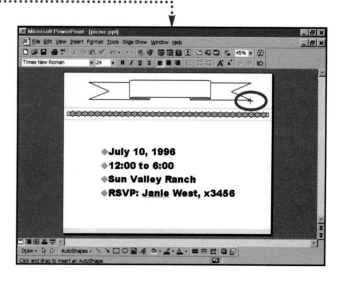

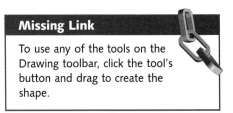

4 To add text to the banner, click the **Text Box** button. Click on the banner and drag to create a text box on top of it.

Missing Link
To use any of the tools on the Drawing toolbar, click the tool's button and drag to create the shape.

5 Type your message. You can use the buttons on the Formatting toolbar to change the font, size, or attributes of the text if you like. When you finish, click anywhere in the slide or press the **Esc** key to deselect the text box.

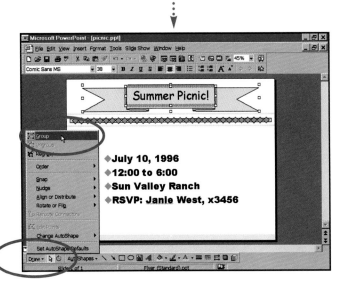

6 You can group the two objects together to make positioning them on the slide easier. Click the text box, and handles appear to show that it's selected. Press and hold the **Shift** key as you click the banner. Handles appear around the banner. Click the **Draw** button on the Drawing toolbar, and select **Group**. ■

Puzzled?
You can resize both objects at one time by dragging a handle. To ungroup the objects so you can work on them separately, click on the group, then click the **Draw** button and select **Ungroup**.

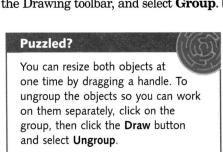

PART IV

Creating an Organization Chart

PEOPLE LOVE TO LOOK AT ORGANIZATION CHARTS, or *org charts,* as they are sometimes called. An org chart is universally understood: It shows the specific position each person holds within a company and who each person reports to (which can be one or more persons). An org chart is an effective means of illustrating a corporate structure, and it's a natural choice for a presentation. And because corporate structures are constantly changing, it's important that you are able to easily create and modify an org chart to keep it updated.

In PowerPoint, you can insert an org chart into any slide using the Microsoft Organization Chart utility program. This program has its own menu and toolbars. Although you open this utility from within PowerPoint, you won't be working in the PowerPoint window when you create your org chart. Instead, you'll be working in the Microsoft Organization Chart utility window. However, you'll still be able to see your PowerPoint presentation behind the org chart window. You can easily switch between the two programs by clicking within the window of the program you want to use or by selecting its button from the Windows 95 taskbar. Once an org chart exists on a slide, opening the Microsoft Organization Chart program is as simple as double-clicking the chart.

Buttons on the Microsoft Organization Chart toolbar enable you to easily add the different types of positions to the chart. Five types of positions can exist within an org chart: subordinate, co-worker (left), co-worker (right), manager, and assistant. These positions show *relationships between positions* as opposed to the status of the employee within the particular organization. (So if an important person in a company reports to someone else, she should not be offended if her position is referred to as "subordinate.") You can use these five positions to build the structure of relationships that exist in any organization; in no way do they indicate status or job responsibilities.

Many tasks you'll perform on an org chart use skills you've already learned. For example, to delete a position, you select the object and press the **Delete** key; to move a position, you use drag-and-drop to move the object to a new location.

In this part of the book, you learn how to create an org chart and how to add, delete, and move people within it. You also learn how to change the style used to display a group of people so the relationships between the people are correct. You use *styles* to define relationships between clusters of workers. For example, if you have several people who report to a supervisor as a group, individually, or as members of teams, you use a particular style to define that subgroup.

When you have all the positions in your chart correctly in place, you're ready to move the chart onto the slide and resize it, if necessary. Once your org chart is on a slide, you can print it using PowerPoint's File, Print command. Because an org chart is printed as part of a slide, the Organization Chart program does not have a Print command as other programs do.

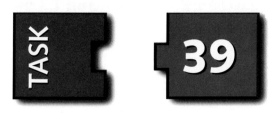

TASK

39

Inserting an Organization Chart on a Slide

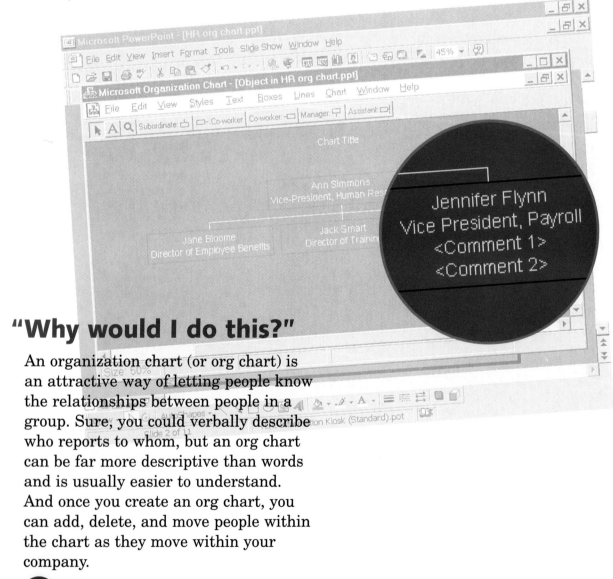

"Why would I do this?"

An organization chart (or org chart) is an attractive way of letting people know the relationships between people in a group. Sure, you could verbally describe who reports to whom, but an org chart can be far more descriptive than words and is usually easier to understand. And once you create an org chart, you can add, delete, and move people within the chart as they move within your company.

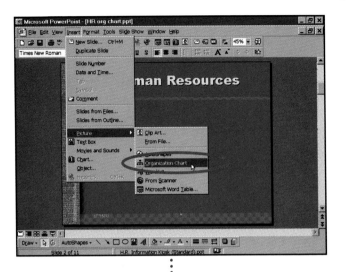

1 Make sure the slide into which you want to insert the org chart is displayed on-screen. Then open the **Insert** menu, select **Picture**, then select **Organization Chart**. The Organization Chart program starts in its own window.

Puzzled?

If Microsoft Organization Chart does not start, then the program has not been installed on your computer. Rerun the setup program to install it.

2 A *placeholder* with the words, Type name here appears highlighted in the highest ranking position on the chart. Type the name you want in the selected box, and press **Enter** to add a job title for that person. If you want, you can add two lines of optional comments by pressing **Enter** after the title line.

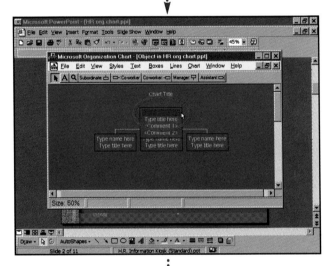

Missing Link

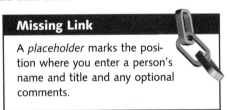

A *placeholder* marks the position where you enter a person's name and title and any optional comments.

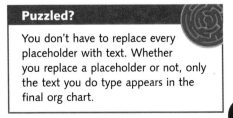

3 Click each additional placeholder that you want to replace with a name and title. Enter the appropriate information, pressing **Enter** to advance from the name to the title and comment lines.

Puzzled?

You don't have to replace every placeholder with text. Whether you replace a placeholder or not, only the text you do type appears in the final org chart.

4 Drag over the placeholder, *Chart Title*, and then type text to replace it, such as **Human Resources Organization Chart**.

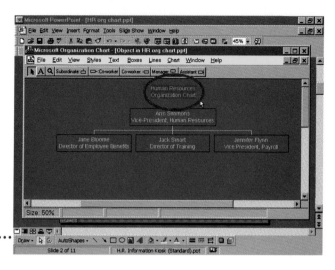

5 When you finish adding people to the org chart, you need to return to the slide. Open the **File** menu and choose **Exit and Return to the** *name of your presentation*. (The name of your presentation appears as part of the command.)

Puzzled?

The Close and Return command is similar to the Exit and Return command. However, Close and Return automatically saves your work; Exit and Return prompts you to save your work before returning to the slide if you haven't already done so.

6 If you haven't saved your work, this dialog box is displayed. Click **Yes** to update the chart on the slide. (Alternatively, you can click **No** to keep the existing chart on the slide the way it is, or you can click **Cancel** to continue working in the Microsoft Organization Chart program.) Once you return to the slide, press **Esc** or click on an open area on the slide to deselect the org chart. ■

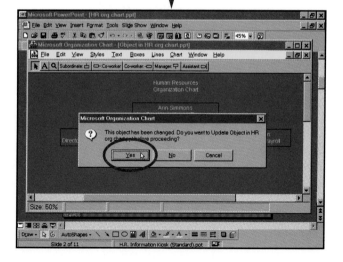

Adding a Person to an Organization Chart

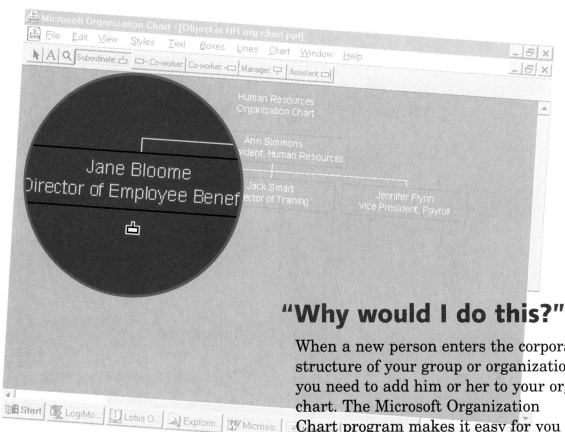

"Why would I do this?"

When a new person enters the corporate structure of your group or organization, you need to add him or her to your org chart. The Microsoft Organization Chart program makes it easy for you to add a new person to a group. And when you add a person to an org chart, the Microsoft Organization Chart program automatically adds the lines to connect that person to others and adjusts the spacing and size of the placeholders as needed.

Task 40: Adding a Person to an Organization Chart

1 Open the Microsoft Organization Chart program by double-clicking on the org chart. Then click the toolbar button for the type of position you want to add (the **Subordinate** button, for example).

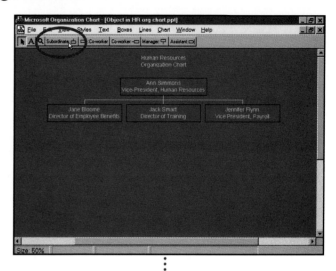

Missing Link

In most organizations, a subordinate works *for* someone, and a co-worker works *with* someone. Generally, an assistant relieves another position of responsibilities.

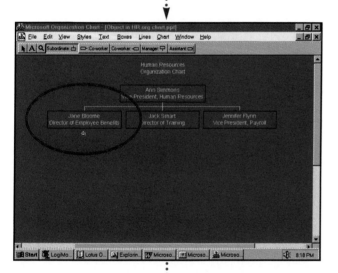

2 The mouse pointer changes to the symbol on the button you clicked. Click the placeholder box for the person in relation to whom you're adding the new position. For example, if you're adding a subordinate for Jane Bloome, you click on Jane's position after you click the Subordinate button.

Puzzled?

To return to a regular mouse pointer, click the **Select** button (the arrow).

3 A placeholder appears for the new position. Type the new person's name and title and any necessary comments, pressing **Enter** to move from one to the next position. ■

Puzzled?

You can continue to add subordinates by repeating steps 1 to 3.

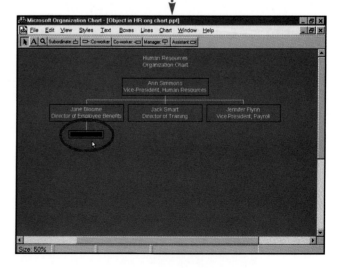

Deleting a Person from an Organization Chart

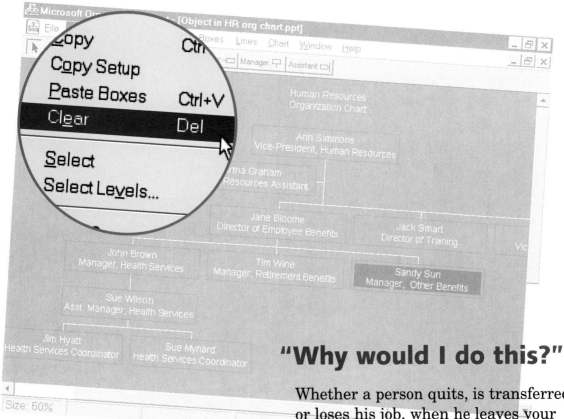

"Why would I do this?"

Whether a person quits, is transferred, or loses his job, when he leaves your group or organization, you have to remove him from your org chart. When you delete a person from an org chart, the Microsoft Organization Chart program automatically fixes the shape and appearance of the chart.

Task 41: Deleting a Person from an Organization Chart

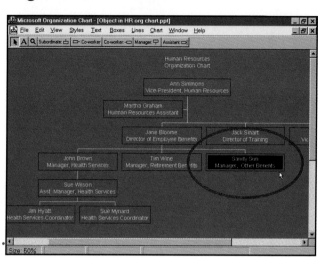

1 With the org chart open, select the position you want to delete by clicking on it.

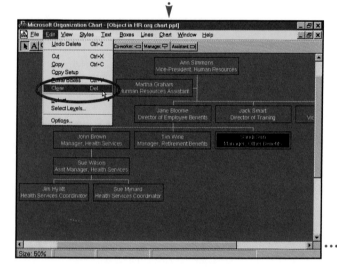

2 Open the **Edit** menu and choose **Clear**, or press the **Delete** key. Microsoft Organization Chart deletes the selected position.

> **Puzzled?**
>
> If you delete a position accidentally, choose the **Edit**, **Undo Delete** command immediately to get it back.

3 When you delete a position, the program automatically adjusts the chart to fill in the gap. ■

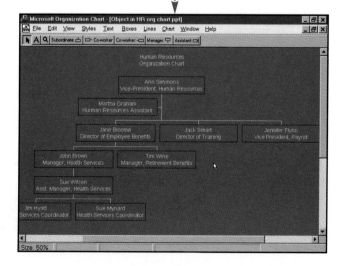

Moving People in an Organization Chart

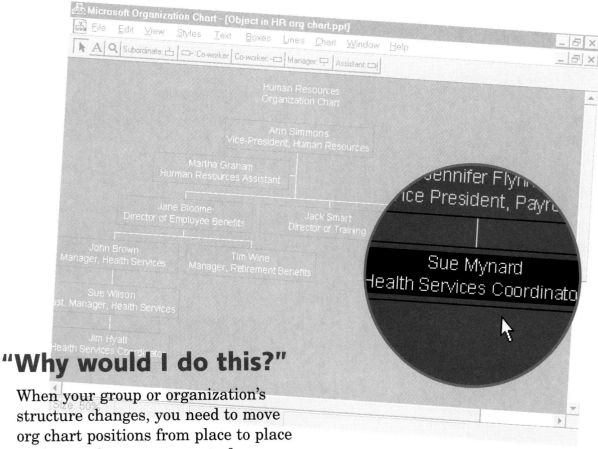

"Why would I do this?"

When your group or organization's structure changes, you need to move org chart positions from place to place or change the arrangement of groups of people accordingly. The power of an org chart program lies in its flexibility. Because people within a corporation often receive promotions or take on new responsibilities, it's important for you to be able to update your org chart easily.

Task 42: Moving People in an Organization Chart

1 With your org chart open, click on the position you want to move. Then drag it on top of the placeholder for the position to whom the selected position now reports. As you drag the position, its outline moves, and the mouse pointer takes on the shape of the position's new relationship.

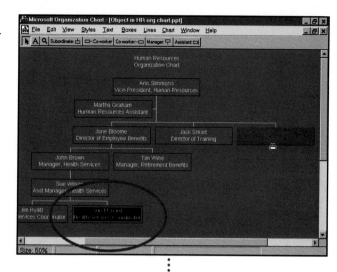

Puzzled?

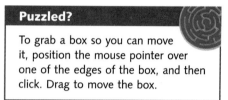

To grab a box so you can move it, position the mouse pointer over one of the edges of the box, and then click. Drag to move the box.

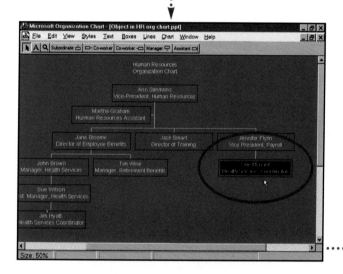

2 When the outline reaches the new location, release the mouse button. The program moves the position to its new location and adjusts the org chart as necessary.

3 Press the **Esc** key or click on an open area of the chart to deselect the position. ■

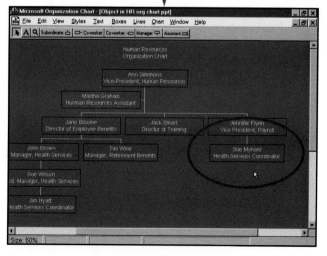

Changing Relationships Within Groups

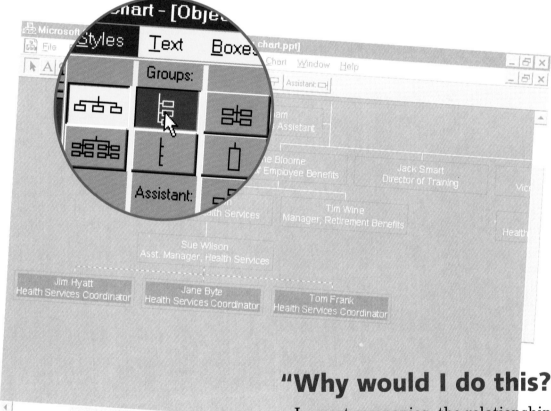

"Why would I do this?"

In most companies, the relationships between persons within departments and among groups are constantly changing and being redefined. Of course, you need to keep those relationships updated in your org chart. Microsoft Organization Chart makes it easy to change relationships between people and their positions.

1 To change the relationship between two persons in a group (persons at the same level within a chart), double-click any member of the group. The whole group appears selected.

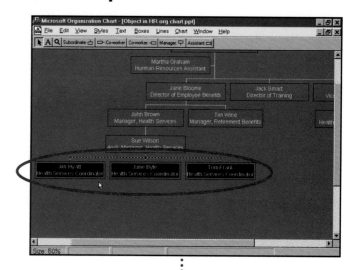

Missing Link

You can also select multiple group members by holding down the **Shift** key and clicking each group member, or by opening the **Edit** menu, choosing **Select**, and then choosing **Group**.

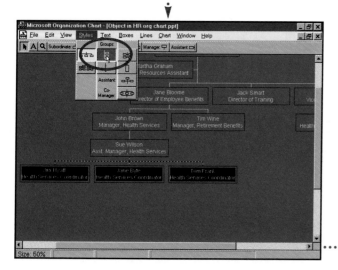

2 Open the **Styles** menu and choose a new group style.

Puzzled?

If you assign a group style and then decide it isn't right, select the group and change the style again, or open the **Edit** menu and select **Undo Chart Style**.

3 The Microsoft Organization Chart program changes the selected group to the style you selected. ■

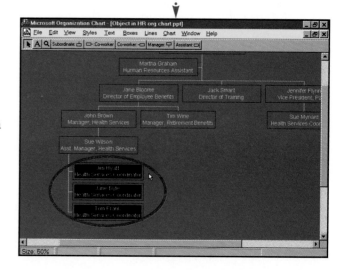

TASK

44

Moving and Resizing an Organization Chart

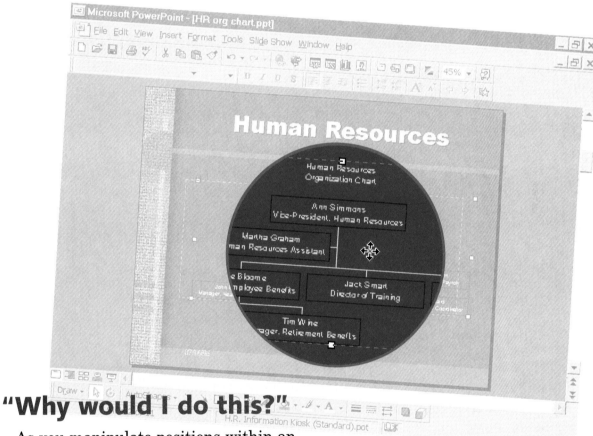

"Why would I do this?"

As you manipulate positions within an org chart, Microsoft Organization Chart makes sure the spacing between positions looks good and the lines connect related placeholders. When you finish with your org chart and insert it in a slide, you might want to make the chart larger or smaller or move it to a different area of the slide.

1 If needed, open the **File** menu and select **Exit and Return to** *Presentation1* to close Microsoft Organization Chart and return to the PowerPoint window. Then, in Slide view, select the org chart by clicking on it. Handles (black or white squares) appear around the chart. To resize an org chart, position the mouse pointer over a corner handle, and the pointer changes to a double-headed arrow.

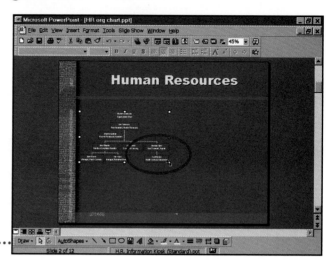

2 When you see the double-headed arrow, click on the chart and drag. An outline of the org chart moves with the mouse pointer as you drag. When the outline is the size you want, release the mouse button.

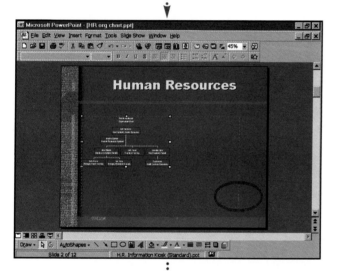

Missing Link

If you want your org chart to be a different size, but remain in proportion, press the **Ctrl** key as you drag the corner handle.

3 To move the org chart, position the mouse pointer over the chart, and the mouse pointer changes to a four-headed arrow and pointer. Click and drag the chart. An outline of the org chart's shape follows the mouse pointer as you drag. When you're satisfied with the new location, release the mouse button, and then press **Esc** to deselect the chart. ■

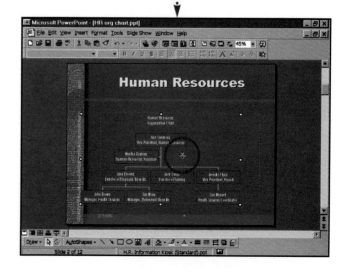

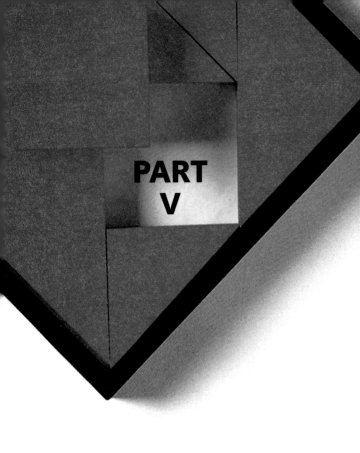

PART V

Working with Tables

SO FAR, YOU'VE ENTERED TEXT ONLY as a title or as information on a slide. Sometimes, however, you want text or numbers in a side-by-side columnar format. Perhaps you have sales data, combinations of text and numbers that should appear side by side, or a list of information that would look great in several columns. This arrangement of data is called a *table*. In PowerPoint, you create a table by using a feature from another program: Microsoft Word for Windows (also called Microsoft Word or just plain Word).

A table is made up of columns and rows, and it can have headers (titles) at the top of each column. When you're working on a table, you can add or delete columns and rows, and you can change the width of a column or the height of a row. You can even make the information in a table bold, italic, or underlined just as you might any other information on a PowerPoint slide.

If you already know how to create a table in Word, you may find this part of the book boring, or you might consider it a welcome review. If you don't know how to create a table in Word, you're in for a treat! A Word table is easy to create, and just as easy to modify and make beautiful.

Because PowerPoint's table feature opens the Word program, it only works if you have Word installed on your computer. You can purchase Word individually or as part of the Microsoft Office suite of programs. If you're unsure whether or not you have Word, click the **Start** button on the Windows 95 taskbar, point to **Programs**, and look for the Microsoft Word program icon. If you see the Word program icon on the menu, Word is already installed on your computer.

In this part of the book, you learn the in's and out's of working with tables. First, you create a table, and then you add information to it. Because all the data in your table isn't going to be the same size, you need to know how to change the width of your columns, which is simple with Word. And even with all the planning in the world, it's possible that you will forget information. So you'll learn how to add and delete columns and rows.

Although using a table means the information in your slide lines up neatly and looks great, that's not the only reason to do it. When you use a table, you can have Word display the information in whatever order you want, such as alphabetical order from A to Z (ascending order) or alphabetically from Z to A (descending order)! Therefore, once you have all the information in your table, you'll learn how to organize and reorganize it. The process of organizing the information in a table is called *sorting*. You can sort a table by one column (last name, for example) or by as many as three columns (last name, first name, and ZIP code, for example).

And finally, after you enter all your information in the table and organize it the way you want it, you can make your table attractive by adding a border to it or by using the Table AutoFormat feature to make it look like you spent hours formatting it. The AutoFormat feature contains preformatted "templates" that include colors, patterns, and character attributes (such as boldface, italics, and underline); the templates are available in both color and black-and-white versions.

TASK 45

Inserting a Table on a Slide

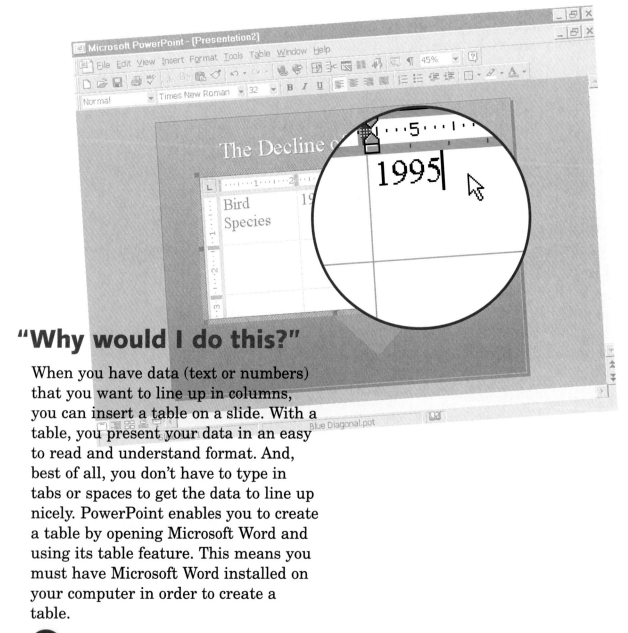

"Why would I do this?"

When you have data (text or numbers) that you want to line up in columns, you can insert a table on a slide. With a table, you present your data in an easy to read and understand format. And, best of all, you don't have to type in tabs or spaces to get the data to line up nicely. PowerPoint enables you to create a table by opening Microsoft Word and using its table feature. This means you must have Microsoft Word installed on your computer in order to create a table.

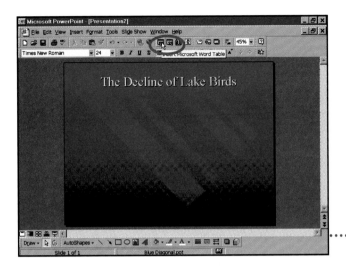

1 In Slide view, display the slide in which you want to insert the table. You might want to use the slide layout for tables which includes a place for a title, like the slide shown here. Then click the **Insert Microsoft Word Table** button.

2 PowerPoint displays a grid that you use to define the number of columns and rows you want in your table. Click and drag over the number of boxes you want in the table. As you drag, the dimensions appear at the bottom of the grid (number of columns × number of rows). When you're satisfied with the dimensions, release the mouse button.

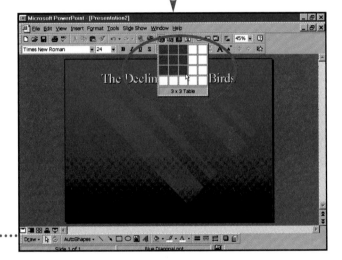

3 A table grid appears on-screen with the number of columns and rows you specified. The cursor appears in the top left *cell*, or box. Enter a title for each column, pressing **Tab** advance to the next cell.

Missing Link

The grid you see surrounding your table will not be visible on your slide.

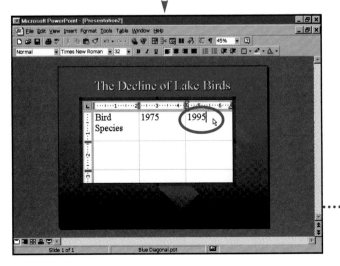

4 After you enter the last column heading, press **Tab** to move to the first row of data. Type data into each cell, pressing **Tab** to move from cell to cell.

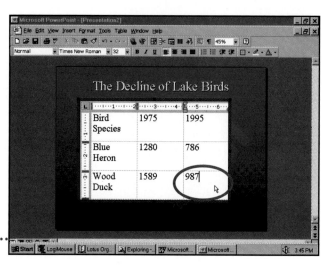

5 When you finish entering the column heads, click anywhere outside the table or press **Esc** to close the Word table and return to PowerPoint's Slide view. The grid disappears, but the table remains selected (as the handles—the tiny white (?) squares—indicate). If you need to move the table, click on it and drag it wherever you need, then release the mouse button.

6 When you're finished adjusting the table, click anywhere outside the table's handles or press **Esc** to deselect the table object. ■

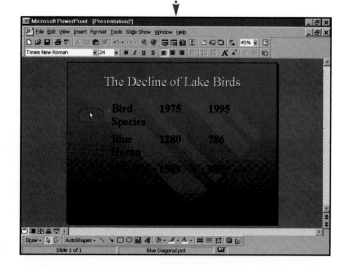

Changing Data in a Table

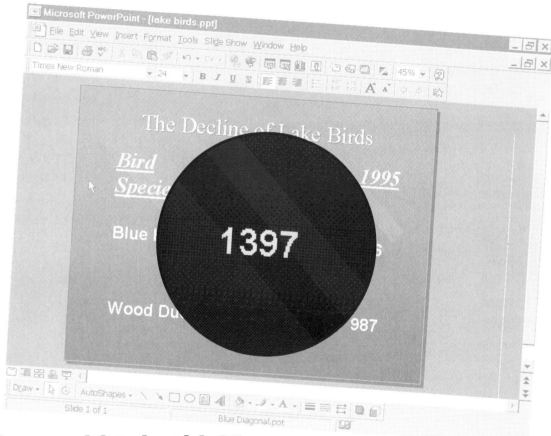

"Why would I do this?"

The information in a table often changes, especially if it is supposed to reflect current data, such as sales figures or market information. In addition to changing the table data, you may want to format it using the techniques you learned in Part II, "Working with Text."

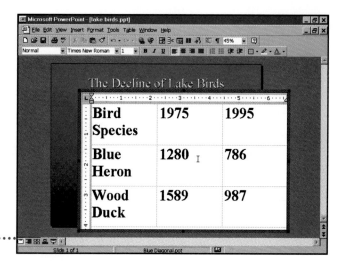

1 To edit the data in a table, double-click it, and the Microsoft Word program starts. Because you're using the Microsoft Word program, the toolbars and menu bars you see now are those of Microsoft Word (not PowerPoint).

2 To change the data in a cell, click in that cell. If your table contains more rows than you can see, use the keyboard's up and down arrow keys to move to the cell. You can erase characters to the right of the cursor by pressing **Delete**. To erase characters to the left of the cursor, press **Backspace** instead.

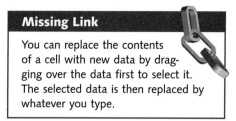

Missing Link

You can replace the contents of a cell with new data by dragging over the data first to select it. The selected data is then replaced by whatever you type.

3 When you're through changing data, click anywhere outside the table, or press **Esc** twice to deselect the table and return to PowerPoint. ■

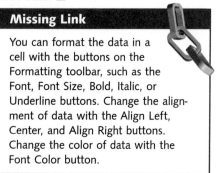

Missing Link

You can format the data in a cell with the buttons on the Formatting toolbar, such as the Font, Font Size, Bold, Italic, or Underline buttons. Change the alignment of data with the Align Left, Center, and Align Right buttons. Change the color of data with the Font Color button.

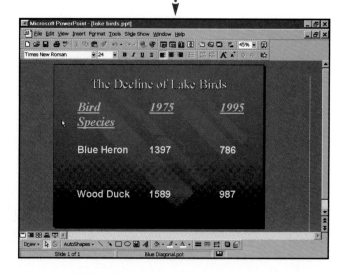

Changing Column and Row Size

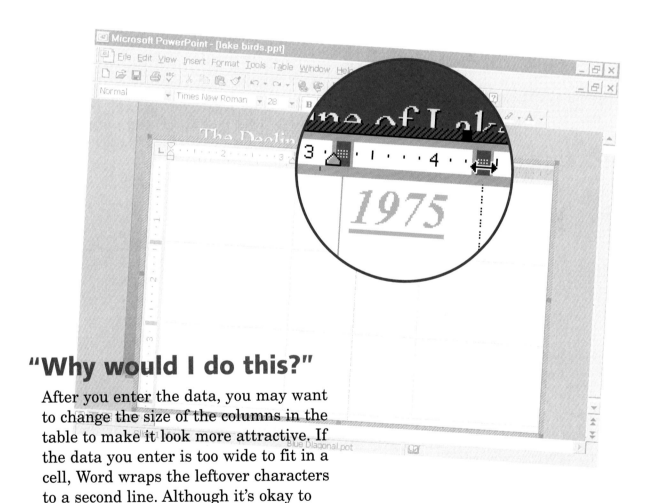

"Why would I do this?"

After you enter the data, you may want to change the size of the columns in the table to make it look more attractive. If the data you enter is too wide to fit in a cell, Word wraps the leftover characters to a second line. Although it's okay to have more than one line of text in a cell, sometimes Word chops a word right in the middle. You can fix that problem by adjusting a column's width.

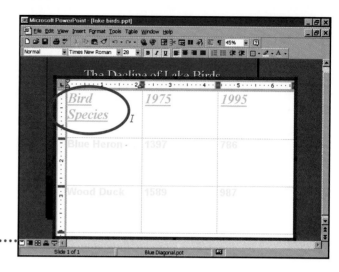

1 Open the Word table if necessary by double-clicking it. The table grid appears.

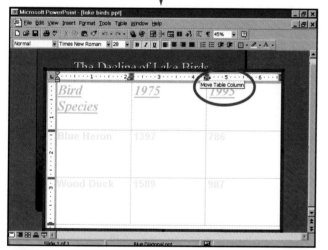

2 To change the width of a column, position the mouse pointer on the ruler at the column divider *to the right* of the column whose width you want to change. The mouse pointer changes to a double-headed arrow, and the words "Move Table Column" appear.

> **Puzzled?**
>
> Sometimes it's hard to make the double-headed arrow appear. Keep moving the mouse pointer around on the table ruler, and eventually you will find it.

3 When the double-headed arrow appears, click and drag the column divider to the left to make the column smaller or to the right to make it bigger. A ghost divider appears, so you can see what the new column width will look like. When you release the mouse button, the column width is adjusted.

> **Missing Link**
>
> If you want to autofit the size of the column to the size of its data, double-click on the column divider. The Cell dialog box appears. Click the **Column** tab, then click **Autofit**.

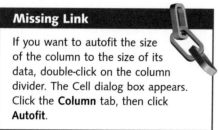

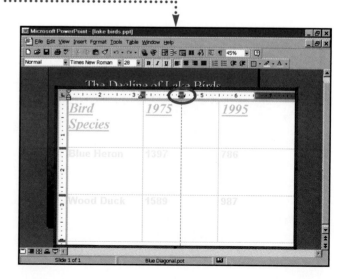

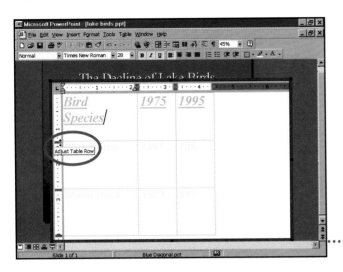

4 You can adjust the height of a row in a similar manner. Position the mouse pointer on the row divider *below* the row whose height you wish to adjust. The words, "Adjust Table Row" appear.

5 Drag the divider downward to make the row bigger, or upward to make it smaller. A ghost divider follows the mouse pointer so you can see what the row's new width will be. Release the mouse button, and the row height is adjusted accordingly.

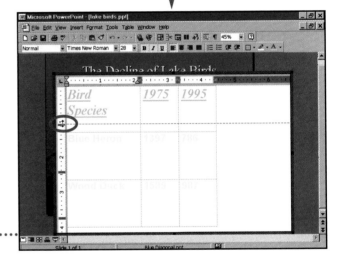

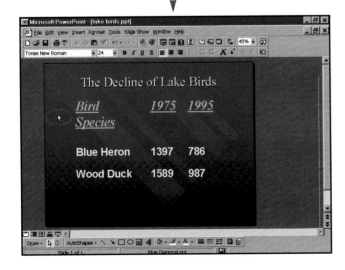

6 When you're done adjusting your table, click anywhere outside the table or press **Esc** twice to deselect it and return to your PowerPoint slide. ■

Inserting and Deleting a Column or Row

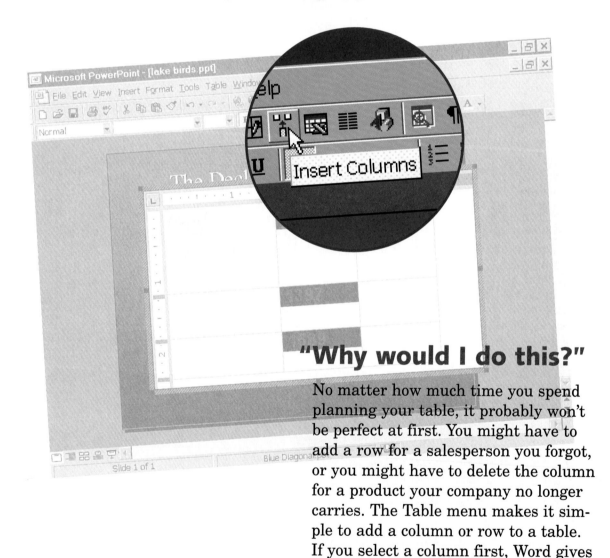

"Why would I do this?"

No matter how much time you spend planning your table, it probably won't be perfect at first. You might have to add a row for a salesperson you forgot, or you might have to delete the column for a product your company no longer carries. The Table menu makes it simple to add a column or row to a table. If you select a column first, Word gives you commands that enable you to insert or delete a column. If you select a row first, the commands enable you to insert or delete a row.

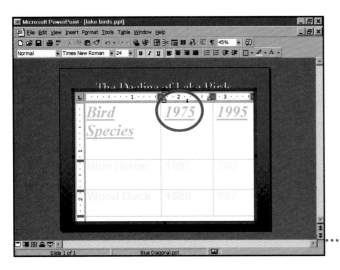

1 Double-click the table if necessary to open it for editing. Position the mouse pointer in the ruler above the column *to the right* of where you want the new column inserted. When the mouse pointer becomes the downward-pointing arrow, click to select the column. To select a row, click in the row *under* which you want to insert a row, then open the **Table** menu and choose **Select Row**.

2 Click the **Insert Columns** or the **Insert Rows** button on the Standard toolbar.

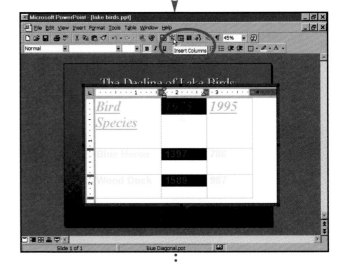

Puzzled?

When you select a column, the **Insert Columns** button appears; when you select a row, the **Insert Row** button appears instead.

Missing Link

You can insert more than one column or row by selecting as many columns or rows as you want to add *before* you click the **Insert** button. Just select one column or row, then drag to select additional columns/rows.

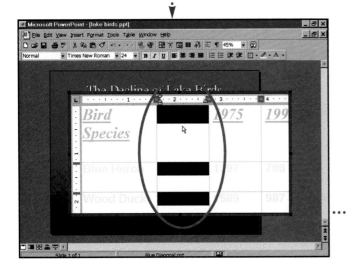

3 A new column appears to the left of the column that you selected. If you inserted a row, then it appears above the row you selected.

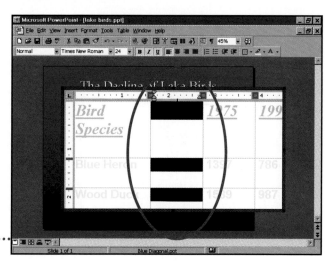

4 To delete a column or row, select it.

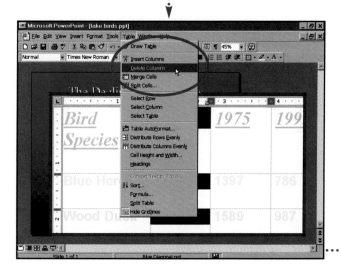

5 Open the **Table** menu and choose **Delete Columns**. (To delete a selected row, open the **Table** menu and choose **Delete Rows**; the selected row disappears from the table.)

6 Word removes the selected columns (or rows) from the table. ■

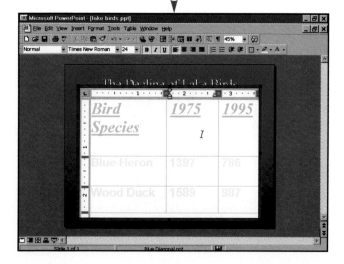

Sorting Data in a Table

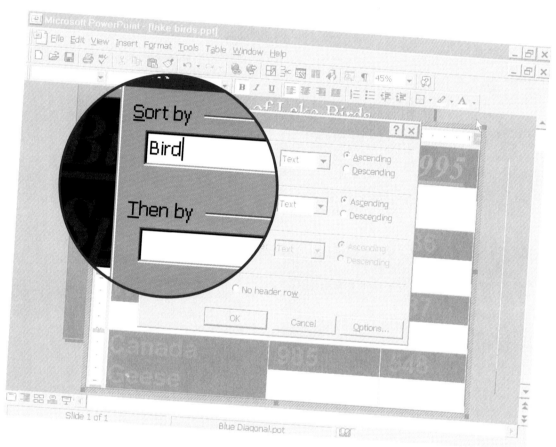

"Why would I do this?"

It's not always easy to make sure you enter your table data in the "right" order. And even if you think it's in the right order, you might have to move things around later. You can sort the contents of a table in ascending or descending order. *Ascending order* arranges the elements in place from

A to Z or 0 to 9; *descending order* arranges the elements in place from Z to A or 9 to 0. You can also sort data by more than one column in your table, so you can sort a list of salespersons by last name and then by first name, just like the names in a phone book.

Task 49: Sorting Data in a Table

1 Double-click to open the table you want to sort. Then open the **Table** menu, and choose **Sort**. The Sort dialog box appears.

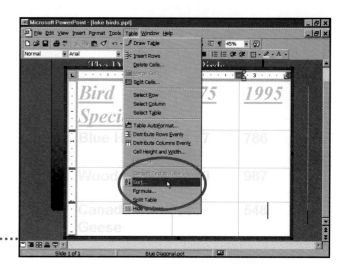

Missing Link

Because Word can sort your data, you can enter it in any order you want to. You don't have to waste time organizing the information; Word does it for you!

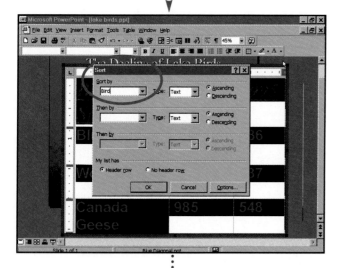

2 Select the column by clicking the **Sort By** drop-down list arrow and selecting the column. Then choose **Ascending** or **Descending** order. (To sort by additional columns, click the **Then by** drop-down list arrow, select the column, and select **Ascending** or **Descending** again.) When you finish entering the sort criteria, click **OK**.

Puzzled?

If the first row in your table contains column names, select the **Header row** option button; if you don't, Word sorts the column names along with your data.

3 Word sorts your table based on the contents of the column(s) you selected. ■

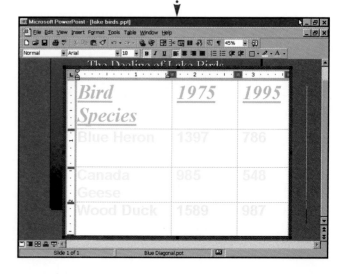

Adding Borders and Shading to a Table

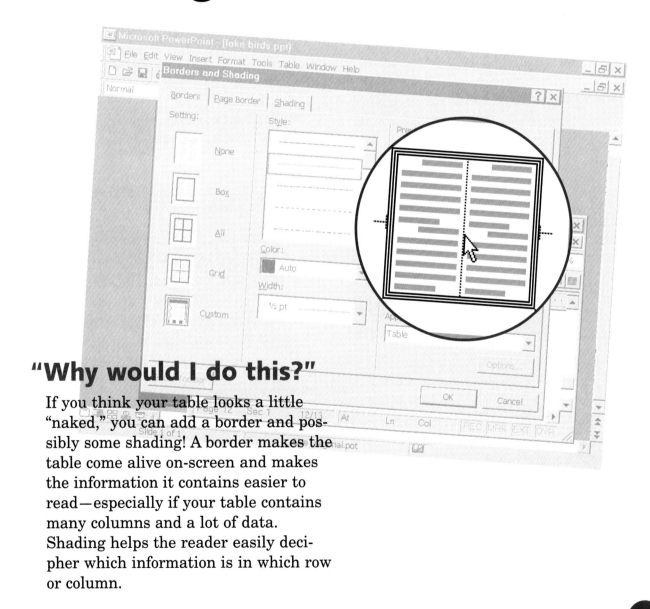

"Why would I do this?"

If you think your table looks a little "naked," you can add a border and possibly some shading! A border makes the table come alive on-screen and makes the information it contains easier to read—especially if your table contains many columns and a lot of data. Shading helps the reader easily decipher which information is in which row or column.

Task 50: Adding Borders and Shading to a Table

1 Open the table you want to enhance by double-clicking it. Then open the **Format** menu and choose **Borders and Shading**. The Table Borders and Shading dialog box appears.

> **Puzzled?**
>
> If you want to format part of a table, such as a row, a column, or a cell, select that part *before* you choose **Borders and Shading**.

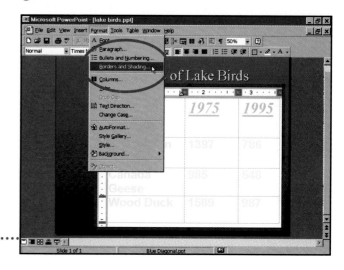

2 Click on the **Borders** tab and select the line style, color, and width that you wish to use.

> **Missing Link**
>
> You can apply a border quickly to the selected area by selecting one from the **Borders** button on the Formatting toolbar.

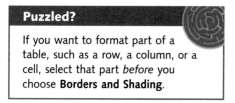

3 Select a **Setting** pattern from the left-hand side of the dialog box, or click the **Preview** diagram to add your border lines. Word displays your selections in the Preview box.

> **Puzzled?**
>
> In the Settings area, None displays the table with no surrounding border or lines between cells. The Box selection surrounds the outside edge with a border. The All selection adds a thick line between columns and rows and outside of the table. The Grid selection does almost the same thing, but the line is thinner than the table border.

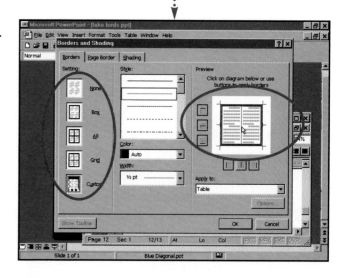

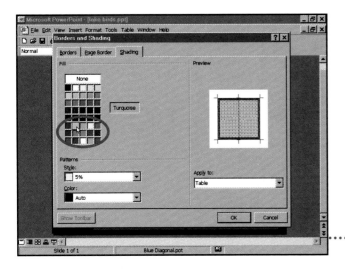

4 Click the **Shading** tab to see the shading options available. If you want a solid background, select a **Fill** color. (As you make your selections, your choices are reflected in the Preview area.)

5 If you want a shaded look, then select a color from the Color list, and select the level of shading you want from the **Style** list.

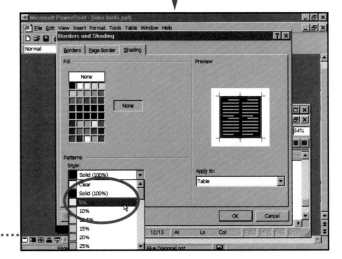

6 When you finish making your selections, click **OK.** Word displays the table with your changes in effect. ■

TASK

51

Using the Table AutoFormat Feature

"Why would I do this?"

Although you can add borders, shading, character formatting, and so on to a table on your own, using Word's Auto-Format feature can save you a lot of time and effort. This "one-stop shopping" tool enables you to apply preformatted table styles easily. Each AutoFormat style contains fonts, attributes, colors, and borders. You can accept each AutoFormat style "as is," or you can turn certain features on or off depending on how you want your table to look.

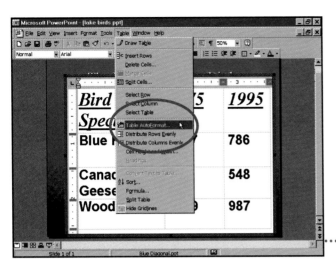

1 Open the table you want to work with by double-clicking on it. Then open the **Table** menu, and choose **Table AutoFormat**. The Table AutoFormat dialog box appears.

2 Select a predesigned pattern from the **Formats** list, and a sample appears in the Preview box. Scroll down the list, selecting patterns, until you find one that creates the effect you want. Then click **OK**.

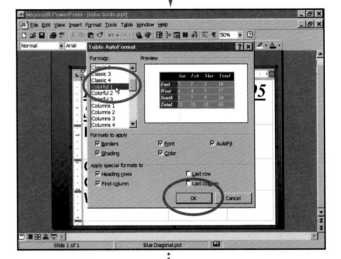

Missing Link

You can turn off part of a pattern by deselecting the options in the **Formats to apply** area. If you don't want to apply the pattern to the top row (the heading row), the last row, or the first or last column, you don't have to. Simply turn those options off in the **Apply special formats to** area.

3 Word applies the Table AutoFormat you selected to the table. (If the table was formatted, that formatting is replaced—unless you turned off the AutoFormat in step 2.) Press the **Esc** key twice to return to the slide and deselect the table. ■

Puzzled?

If you decide you want to get rid of the formatting, choose **Table AutoFormat** from the **Table** menu again, and then click the **None** option in the Formats list, then click **OK** in the Table AutoFormat dialog box.

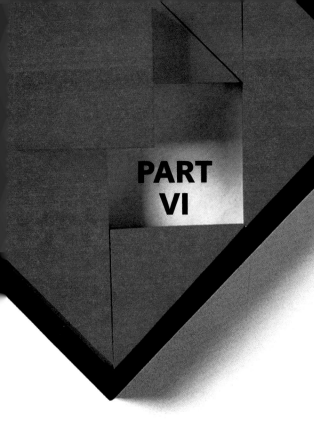

Working with Charts

T'S NOT ALWAYS EASY FOR THE MEMBERS of an audience to read the numbers in your presentations, even if a projector displays the numbers on a large screen. And in addition to being able to read the numbers, your audience has to think about what the numbers represent. It's so much easier to graphically show numbers to your audience! And in PowerPoint, transforming raw numbers into meaningful, attractive charts is simple.

In this part of the book, you'll learn how to insert a chart onto a slide and add data to it. You can add a meaningful title and modify the text within the chart by changing its font, size, and alignment. You'll also learn how to resize and move your chart as needed.

And, because PowerPoint enables you to create a variety of chart types, you'll learn how to change the type of an existing chart. (Creating a chart in PowerPoint is similar to creating a chart using Excel; if you're familiar with that program, this section will be a snap!)

The most often used chart types are column and bar charts, which show how data changes over a period of time. For example, you could use a column or bar chart to show your company's monthly sales during the last year. Column and bar charts have identical uses, but a column chart uses vertical columns, and a bar chart uses horizontal bars. The column chart is the default chart type.

Another common chart type is the pie chart. You use a pie chart to display how smaller elements make up a whole entity. For example, you might use a pie chart to show how your total expenses are divided into their various categories.

A line chart is the best chart type to use when displaying how values change over time, such as profit margins, which might vary from month to month. An area chart is similar to a line chart, except that the area under the line is filled in, in order to emphasize the amount of change.

Most charts consist of an x-axis and a y-axis: the *x-axis* is the horizontal axis, and the *y-axis* is the vertical axis. Data is plotted along these two axes, unless you're creating a pie chart, which has no axis, or a 3-D chart, which also has a z-axis. (The *z-axis* provides depth that gives the added dimensional appearance.) All of PowerPoint's chart types are available as 2-D or 3-D charts. Whereas the 2-D charts have a flatter appearance, the 3-D charts appear to have depth. A 3-D chart looks more dramatic, and you can usually rotate it to get the best view of your data.

Each group of related data in a chart (such as the twelve figures that represent your monthly sales in the Eastern territory) is called a *data series*. Each individual value that's plotted (January's sales figure, for example) is called a *data point*.

If you were to chart the twelve months of sales data for *two* territories (such as Eastern and Southern) then your chart would have two data series. Often, a data series corresponds to a particular *row* of data in a table. If you have more than one data series, you'll have more than one row in your table.

Each data series is divided into categories. For example, if you plotted sales data for each of the twelve months in a year, then each month would be a category. Categories often represent units of time, such as months, years, quarters, etc. Typically, a category corresponds to a particular *column* of data in a table. For example, the sales amount for each month would be entered into a different column.

Gridlines (which are typically displayed horizontally) from the y-axis, help you identify a particular data point's value. You can turn gridlines off if you don't like them.

A legend helps to define the various elements in a chart. For example, in a pie chart, a legend helps the viewer decipher what each part of the pie stands for. You do not have to include a legend in your chart, although they can sometimes be very helpful.

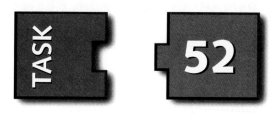

Inserting a Chart on a Slide

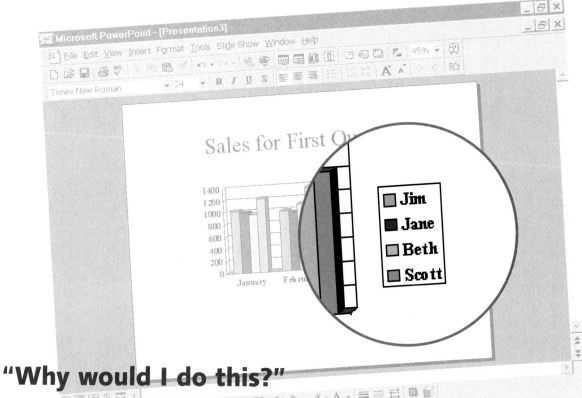

"Why would I do this?"

A chart presents data in a graphical format so that people are better able to see trends in data and pick up on the point you are making. By turning numeric data into a chart, you can make the data (and your audience) come alive. And when you use a chart on a slide, you don't have to worry about your numbers being small and illegible—as they often are in traditional (boring) presentations.

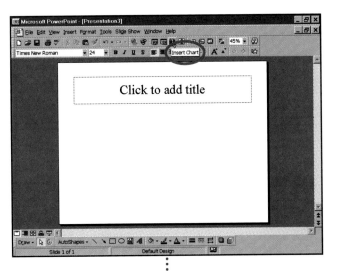

1 In Slide View, open the slide on which you want to insert a chart. Click the **Insert Chart** button. PowerPoint opens a datasheet (table), which you use to enter your chart data and create the chart.

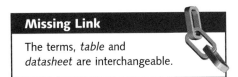

Missing Link

The terms, *table* and *datasheet* are interchangeable.

2 The data displayed in the datasheet is fake—it's there so you can see how to enter your own data correctly (by simply following the example). When you enter data into each cell (box) it replaces the sample data. Click on the cell that contains the word, "1st Qtr," and type the name of a category. Press the **right arrow** to move to the next cell. Continue until you've entered all your categories.

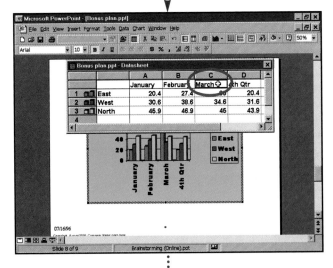

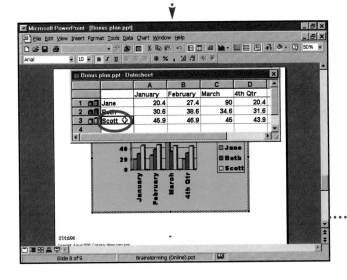

3 Click on the cell that contains the word, "East," and enter the name of your first data series. If your table contains more than one data series, press the **down arrow** to move to the cell that contains "West." Continue until you've entered all your data series names.

4 Now enter the information for your chart. Click in a cell and type the information you want there. You can use the arrow keys to move from cell to cell, or you can click with your mouse.

Missing Link

To make the datasheet larger, position the mouse pointer over the lower-right corner of the window where it changes to a double-headed arrow, press and hold the left mouse button, and drag.

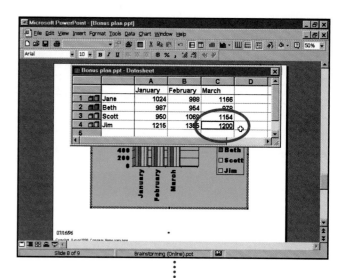

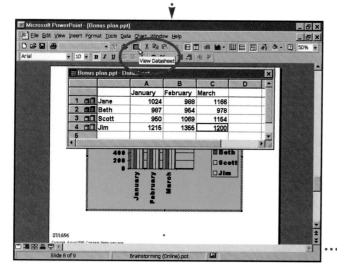

5 When you finish entering your data and you're ready to remove the datasheet so you can see your chart, click the **View Datasheet** button *to turn it off*. View Datasheet is a *toggle* button. When it's enabled (it appears to be pushed in), you see the datasheet grid. When it's not enabled, you see the chart.

6 PowerPoint assumes that your data series were entered in rows, and your categories in columns. If you entered your data series in columns, then click the **By Column** button. When you switch the view, the data currently displayed on the x-axis and the legend change places. Press the **Esc** key twice to return to the slide and deselect the chart. ■

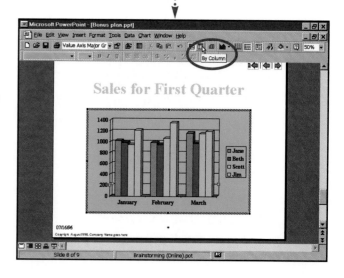

Changing and Adding Chart Data

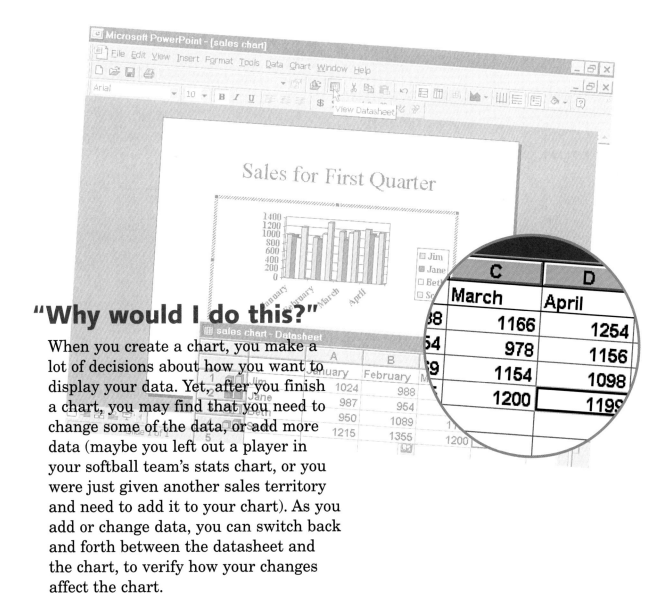

"Why would I do this?"

When you create a chart, you make a lot of decisions about how you want to display your data. Yet, after you finish a chart, you may find that you need to change some of the data, or add more data (maybe you left out a player in your softball team's stats chart, or you were just given another sales territory and need to add it to your chart). As you add or change data, you can switch back and forth between the datasheet and the chart, to verify how your changes affect the chart.

Task 53: Changing and Adding Chart Data

1 Open the chart by double-clicking on it. A thatched border surrounds the chart. Click the **View Datasheet** button to switch back to the datasheet grid, in which you enter additional data.

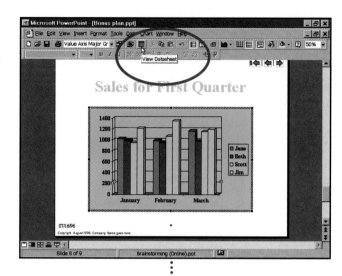

Missing Link

The range of data you enter determines the scale that the y-axis uses.

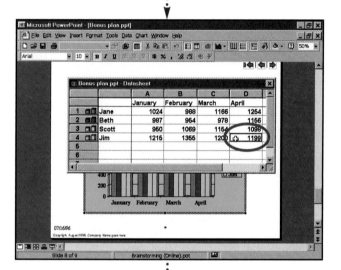

2 To change data, simply click in the cell and type the new data. To add data, click an empty cell in the next available column or row and type your data.

Missing Link

Use the arrow keys to move from cell to cell to enter your data, or click on a cell.

3 As you enter data, the chart under the datasheet is adjusted to reflect your changes. To remove the datasheet so you can see the chart, click the **View Datasheet** button again. ■

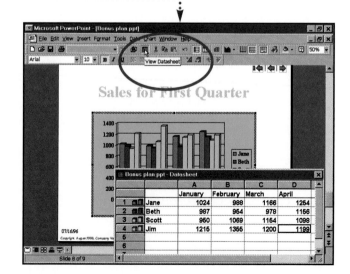

Puzzled?

If you don't like the column chart (which is the default style), choose another chart style as explained in Task 56.

Modifying Chart Text

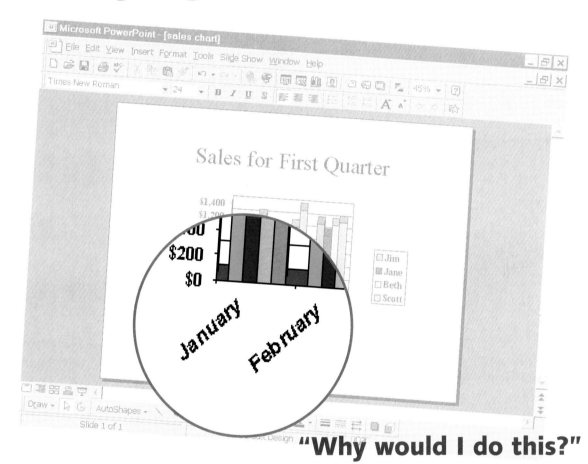

"Why would I do this?"

Microsoft Graph does a terrific job of creating a chart, but sometimes the text in the chart doesn't look quite the way you want it to. For example, the point size of column text may be too large for the number of columns in your chart. No problem! You can modify the fonts in the chart and their sizes. You can also change the alignment of the text from horizontal to vertical.

Task 54: Modifying Chart Text

1 Double-click the chart to open it, and then click on any text you want to modify. For example, to change the size or font of the labels on the category axis, click on one of the labels. Optionally, you can select the object you wish to modify from the **Chart Objects** list on the Standard toolbar. For example, you can select **Category Axis**. Microsoft Graph displays handles at either end of the axis you select.

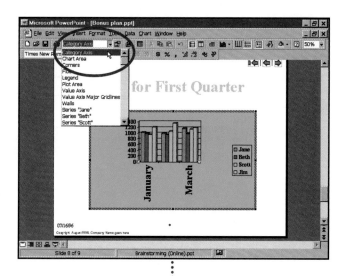

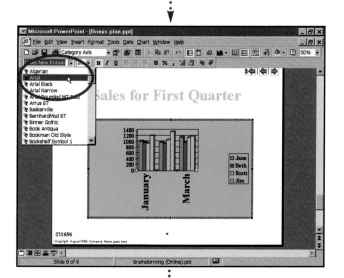

2 To change the font of the selected labels, choose a font from the **Font** list on the formatting toolbar. To change the size of the label text, choose a point size from the **Font Size** list.

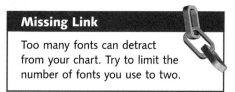

Missing Link

Too many fonts can detract from your chart. Try to limit the number of fonts you use to two.

3 You can add bold, italic, or underline attributes to the selected labels by clicking the appropriate button on the Formatting toolbar. For example, click the **Italic** button.

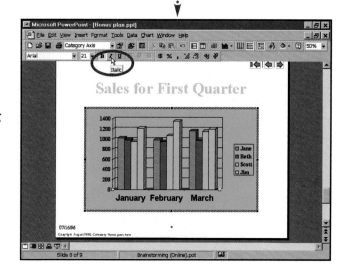

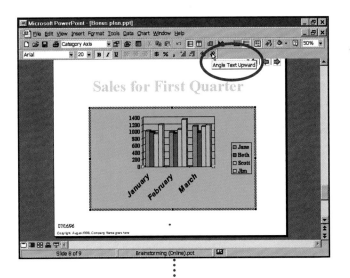

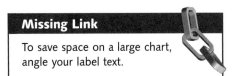

4 You can change the orientation of the selected labels by clicking either the **Angle Text Upward** or the **Angle Text Downward** button on the Formatting toolbar.

Missing Link

To save space on a large chart, angle your label text.

5 You can change the format of the numbers of the value axis by selecting **Value Axis** from the Chart Objects list, then clicking a number style button on the Formatting toolbar, such as the **Currency Style** button, the **Percent Style** button, or the **Comma Style** button.

Puzzled?

You can change the color of your labels by opening the **Format** menu, selecting **Font**, then selecting the color you wish and clicking **OK**.

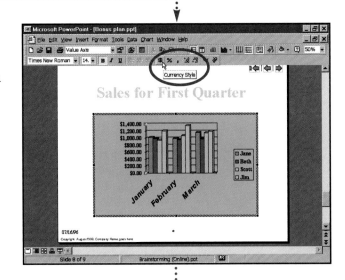

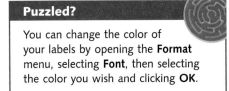

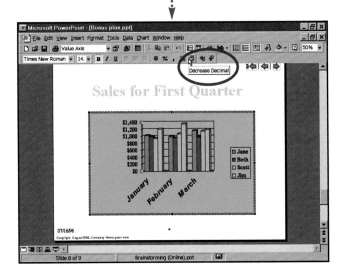

6 To decrease the number of decimals used in the value labels, click the **Decrease Decimal** button on the Formatting toolbar. To increase the number of decimals, click the **Increase Decimal** button instead. You can click these buttons multiple times, as needed, to display the number of decimal places you desire. When you're through making changes to your chart, press **Esc** twice to return to your PowerPoint slide. ■

169

Changing the Chart Type

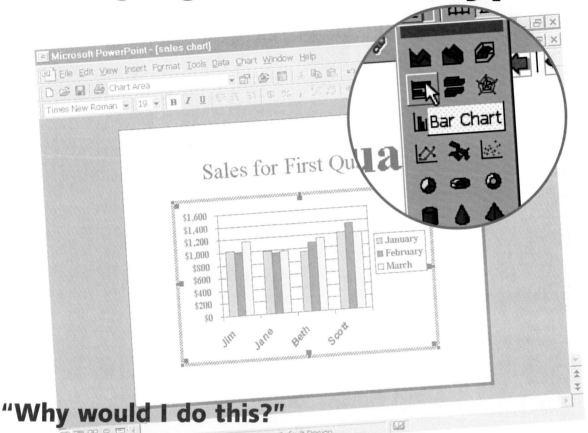

"Why would I do this?"

Microsoft Graph offers a wide variety of chart types. When you first create a chart, Microsoft Graph uses the column chart type by default. However, the program enables you to change the chart to whatever type you want. For example, you may want to use a different type of chart to show off your data better, or you may want to show your data in two different ways.

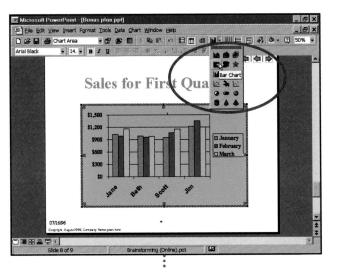

1 Double-click the chart to open it. Click the arrow next to the **Chart Type** button on the Standard toolbar. In the palette list that appears, click the chart type you want to use.

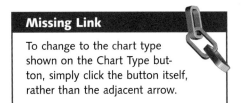

Missing Link

To change to the chart type shown on the Chart Type button, simply click the button itself, rather than the adjacent arrow.

2 Microsoft Graph applies the new chart type to your data and displays it in the chart window.

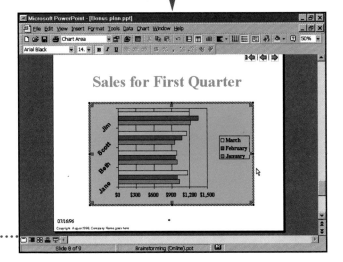

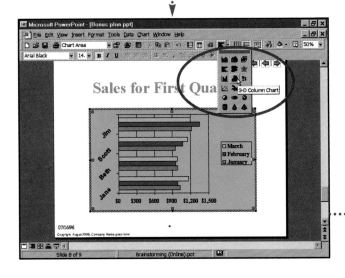

3 If you select a 3-D chart from the Chart Type list, you can change how the chart looks by rotating it. By rotating the chart, you can emphasize a particular data series by making it more visible. (Likewise, you can de-emphasize a series by making it less visible.)

Task 55: Changing the Chart Type

4 To rotate the chart, position the mouse cursor at the lower-right corner. The handle under it turns into a "+", and the word, "Corners" appears.

> **Missing Link**
>
> Finding the corners on a chart can be tricky because they often blend in with the chart background.

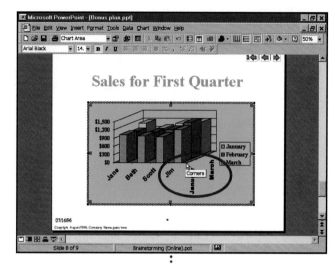

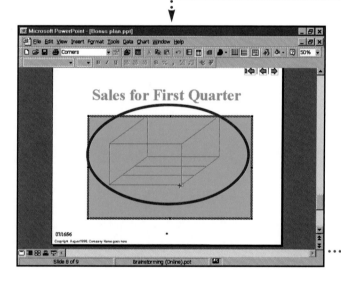

5 Click and drag the mouse pointer. The chart disappears, and in its place you see a 3-D outline that rotates as you drag the mouse pointer.

6 Release the mouse button when you're satisfied with the chart's new position. The chart is rotated to the position you selected. ■

> **Puzzled?**
>
> If you're not happy with the rotated chart, click the **Undo** button on the Standard toolbar.

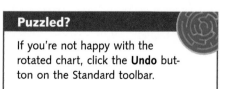

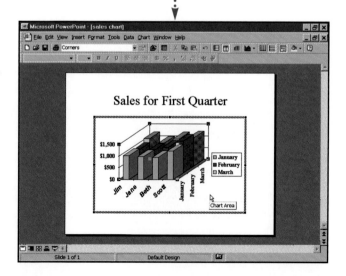

Changing Chart Options

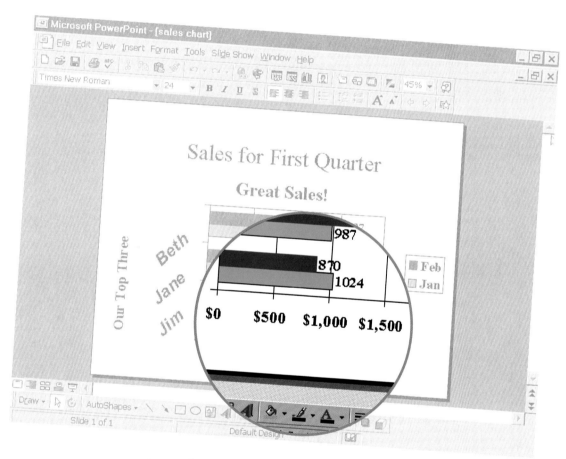

"Why would I do this?"

The chart options allow you to add a title to your chart, or to the value (y) axis and the category (x) axis. Adding titles helps your viewers identify what data is being charted. In addition, the chart options allow you to add gridlines to help your viewers determine the value of a particular data point. Also, you can opt to display (or not display) a legend, data labels (labels which identify each column, bar, line, etc.), or a data table (the table of data from which the chart was plotted).

Task 56: Changing Chart Options

1 Double-click the chart to open it. Open the **Chart** menu and choose **Chart Options**. The Chart Options dialog box appears.

> **Puzzled?**
>
> The Chart Options dialog box contains many pages on which you can change many elements of your chart. To change from page to page, click a tab.

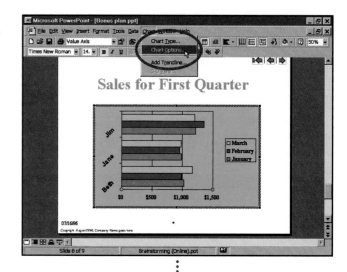

2 On the **Axes** tab, you can turn off the x or y axis labels if you like. This might be a good idea if a chart is crowded with labels and data, as a 3-D chart often is.

> **Missing Link**
>
> Often, the axis labels are the only things which enable a viewer to understand your data, so be careful about turning them off.

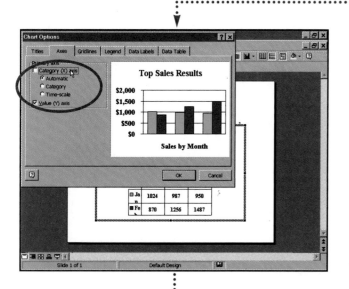

3 On the **Gridlines** tab, you can add minor gridlines to the Value axis (extra lines between the major gridlines), turn off gridlines, or display gridlines from the Category (x) axis. On a line chart like this, turning both X and Y gridlines on enables the viewer to see the data points more clearly.

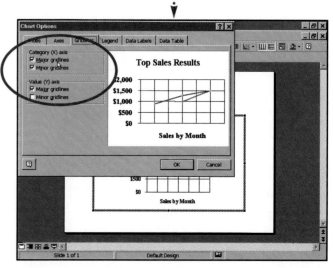

4 On the **Legend** tab, you can choose exactly where you want the legend displayed (if at all). To turn the legend display off, click the **Show legend** option to deselect it. To move the position of the legend, select an area from the list. On this chart, the legend appears at the top.

Missing Link

A legend is important in charts with several data series, since they help the viewer identify what each series stands for.

5 On the **Data Labels** tab, you can add value labels (to help identify the exact value of a particular data point—handy in a pie chart like this one), and/or category labels (to help identify each category). If you show the legend key next to a label, the legend symbol (the color) for that data series appears next to the label. (Notice also that all six tabs do not appear when you select a pie chart.)

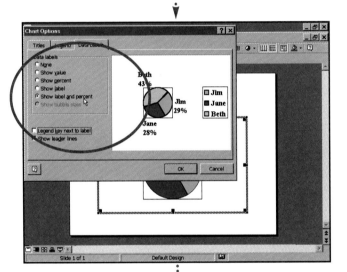

6 On the **Data Table** tab, you can opt to display the datasheet, shown here with a column chart. When you're through selecting chart options, click **OK**. The chart changes to reflect the options you selected. ■

Missing Link

Display the data table on charts where you want to review the data carefully during your presentation.

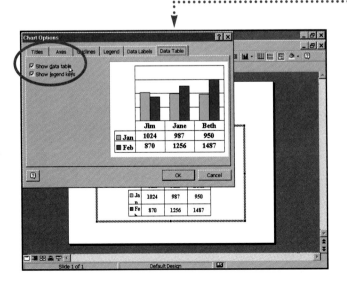

Resizing a Chart

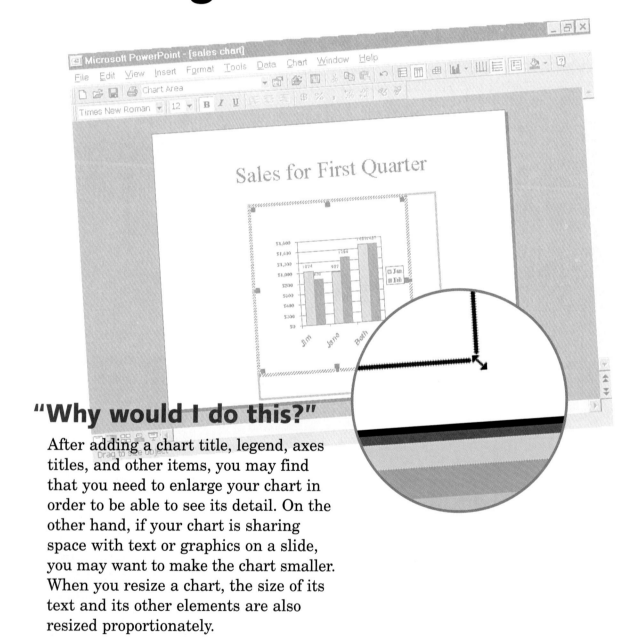

"Why would I do this?"

After adding a chart title, legend, axes titles, and other items, you may find that you need to enlarge your chart in order to be able to see its detail. On the other hand, if your chart is sharing space with text or graphics on a slide, you may want to make the chart smaller. When you resize a chart, the size of its text and its other elements are also resized proportionately.

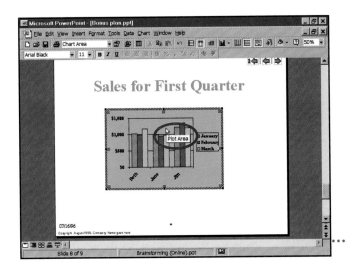

1 Double-click on the chart to open it. A hashed outline appears around the chart.

2 Position the mouse pointer over one of the corners of the chart so it changes to a two-headed arrow. Drag the corner outward to make the chart bigger; drag it inward to make the chart smaller. A ghostly outline of the chart follows the mouse pointer so you can see what its new size will be.

Missing Link

By dragging a corner to resize your chart, you'll be assured of maintaining its proportions. You can resize your chart by dragging a side handle, but keep in mind that your text may no longer be proportional.

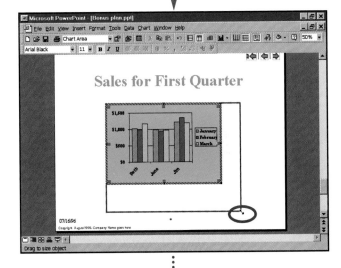

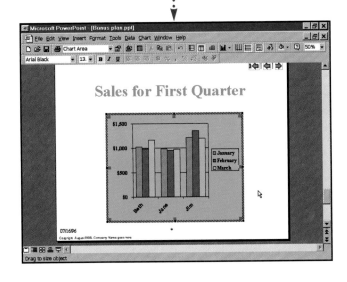

3 Release the mouse button, and the chart is resized to fit the ghostly outline. Press **Esc** twice to return to your PowerPoint slide. ■

Puzzled?

If you need to move the chart after resizing it, press **Esc** once, and the chart will remain selected. Click the chart and drag it, then release the mouse button.

Moving a Chart

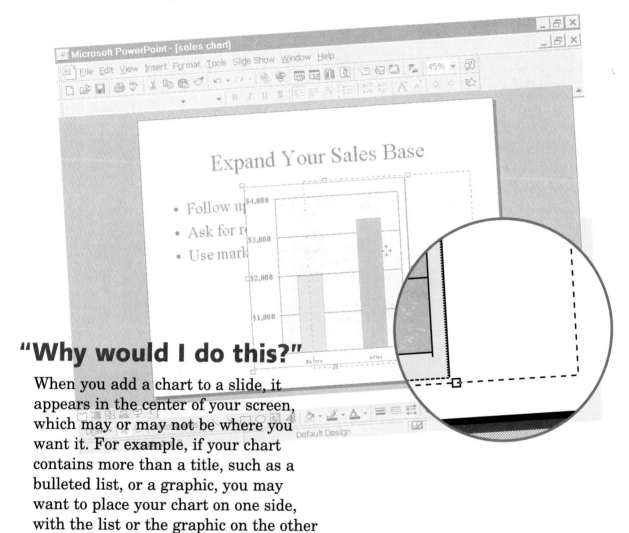

"Why would I do this?"

When you add a chart to a slide, it appears in the center of your screen, which may or may not be where you want it. For example, if your chart contains more than a title, such as a bulleted list, or a graphic, you may want to place your chart on one side, with the list or the graphic on the other side. Also, if you've just resized your chart, it may no longer be in the right spot. In either case, it's simple to move your chart exactly where you'd like it to be.

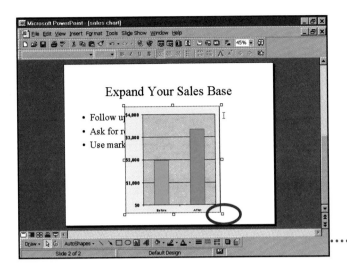

1 Click once on the chart to select it. Handles (small white squares) appear around the chart. Double-click on the chart to open it. A hashed outline appears around the chart.

2 Position the mouse pointer over the chart. The mouse pointer changes to a four-headed arrow. Drag the chart on the slide to its new location. A ghostly outline of the chart follows the mouse pointer so you can see where you're placing it.

Puzzled?

You can move a chart over the top of some slide text or a graphic, and it will show through the chart background, as long as you have not changed its color.

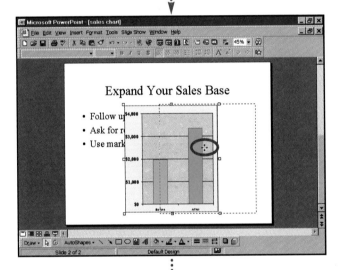

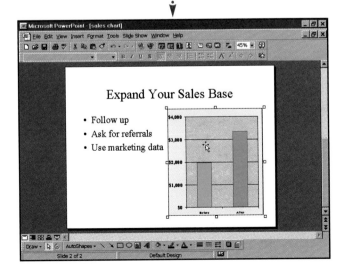

3 Release the mouse button, and the chart is moved to the location you indicated. Press **Esc** twice to return to your PowerPoint slide. ■

PART VII

Working in Outline View

S O FAR, YOU'VE WORKED EXCLUSIVELY in the graphical world of slides. You've created and edited individual slides and added text, colors, patterns, artwork, tables, and charts. While you were working on each slide, you knew exactly how that slide would look.

PowerPoint's Outline View enables you to view your slides in a text-only format so you can analyze your text without having the distractions of slide backgrounds and graphic images. Next to each line of text on the outline is either a slide number and icon (which appears in front of the title for each slide in your presentation) or a bullet (which appears in front of the text within a slide).

Although no graphic images appear in Outline View, you can still tell if a slide contains graphics by looking at the slide's icon (which appears next to the slide title). A slide which contains something other than text (such as a graphic or a chart) has an icon with a small graphic image on it, while a slide containing only text has a blank icon. In addition, Outline View has its own toolbar that enables you to move slides up and down within the presentation. (You can also use the drag-and-drop techniques to move slides within an outline.)

You edit slide text in Outline View in much the same way you edit text in Slide View. After you select the text, you can delete or replace it using regular mouse or keyboard editing techniques. If you add, edit, or move text in Outline View, those changes appear on your slides when you switch to any other view. And although you won't see any graphic images on your slides, you will see text formatting (such as boldface, italics, and underlining) unless you choose to turn the formatting off.

Outline View makes it easy to rearrange things in your presentation. You can use drag and drop or the buttons on the Outline toolbar to change the order of the slides. The real advantage of Outline View, however, is that it enables you to reorganize your presentation. Either by using drag-and-drop techniques or by using the buttons on the Outline toolbar, you can change the position of text—whether that text is a bulleted item, or a slide title. The following table describes the Outline toolbar buttons:

Outline Toolbar Buttons

Button	Description	Use
	Promote	Makes a text line more important by decreasing the amount of indention.
	Demote	Makes a text line less important by increasing the amount of indention.
	Move Up	Moves a text line up one position.
	Move Down	Moves a text line down one position.
	Collapse	Hides the details in the selected slide so only the slide title appears.
	Expand	Displays the details in the selected slide so all the slide contents display.
	Collapse All	Hides the details of all the slides in a presentation, displaying only the slide titles.
	Expand All	Displays the details of all the slides in a presentation.
	Summary Slide	Creates a summary slide (agenda) listing the titles of selected slides.
	Show Formatting	Hides/Displays the formatting used in slides.

In this part, you learn to use Outline View to organize your presentation so the slides and the text within each slide progress logically.

Selecting a Slide in Outline View

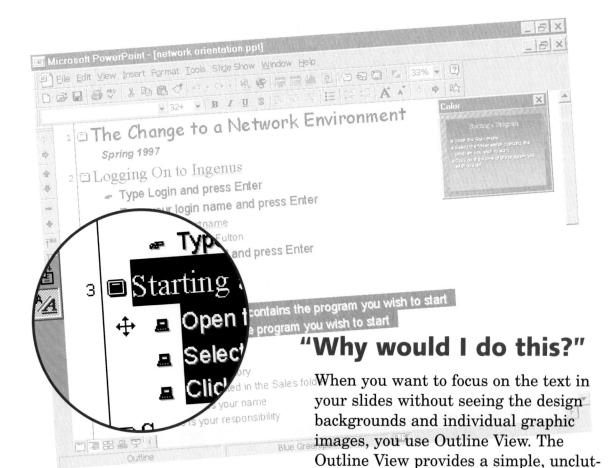

"Why would I do this?"

When you want to focus on the text in your slides without seeing the design backgrounds and individual graphic images, you use Outline View. The Outline View provides a simple, uncluttered work area in which you can edit text within slides and change the order of the text and slides. However, before you can work with a slide's text, you must select the slide.

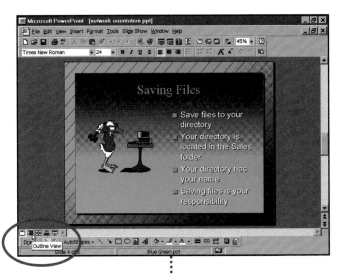

1 From any PowerPoint view (and with any slide visible), click the **Outline View** button. The slides in your presentation are listed in an outline form.

> **Missing Link**
>
> Although the Standard and Formatting toolbars remain visible, Outline View displays its own toolbar along the left side of the window. The tools on the Outline toolbar enable you to move, hide, and display the text on your slides.

2 When you switch to Outline View, the slide you were viewing in the previous view becomes the selected slide automatically. To make a different slide the active slide, position the mouse pointer over the slide icon of the slide you wish to select. The pointer changes to a four-headed arrow. With the four-headed arrow pointer, click on the icon of the slide you want to select.

> **Missing Link**
>
> A view of the selected slide appears in the Color window.

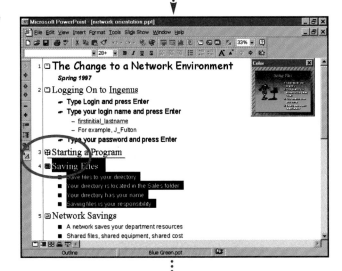

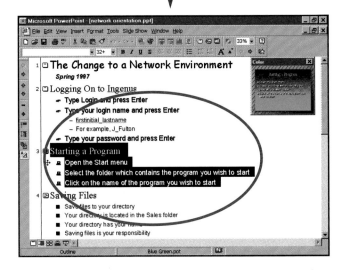

3 When you select a slide, the entire slide—including all the detail text—appears highlighted. To select a group of slides, click the first slide, then press and hold the Shift key as you click on the last slide icon in the group. ■

> **Puzzled?**
>
> If the icon to the right of the slide number is empty, the slide does not contain graphics; if the icon has shapes on it, the slide does contain graphic images, or a chart.

Hiding and Displaying Data

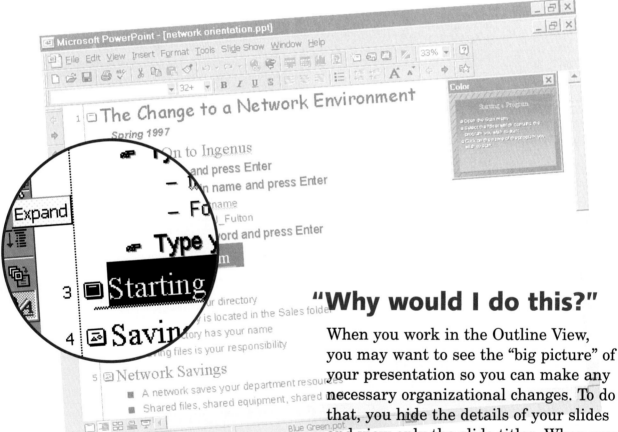

"Why would I do this?"

When you work in the Outline View, you may want to see the "big picture" of your presentation so you can make any necessary organizational changes. To do that, you hide the details of your slides and view only the slide titles. When you finish looking at the big picture, you simply tell PowerPoint to display the details again. You can hide and display details on one or more selected slides (as explained in steps 1–3) or in all the slides (as explained in steps 4 and 5).

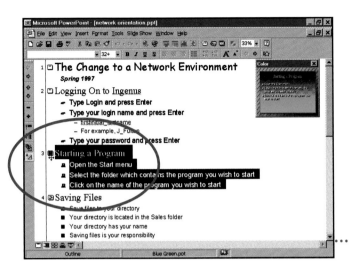

1 Select the slide or slides for which you want to hide the details.

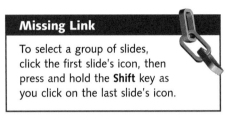

Missing Link

To select a group of slides, click the first slide's icon, then press and hold the **Shift** key as you click on the last slide's icon.

2 Click the **Collapse** button on the Outline toolbar to hide details for the selected slide(s).

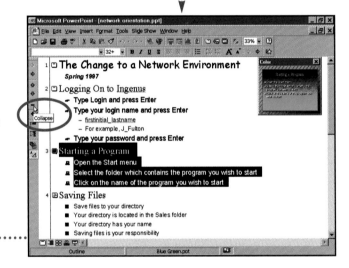

3 PowerPoint indicates that a slide has hidden details by underlining it. To display the hidden details for the selected slide(s), click the **Expand** button on the Outline toolbar.

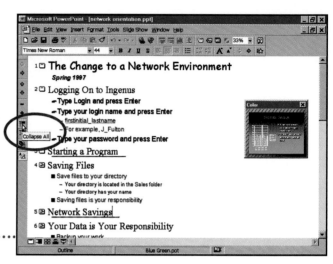

4 To hide the details for all the slides in your presentation, click on the **Collapse All** button on the Outline toolbar.

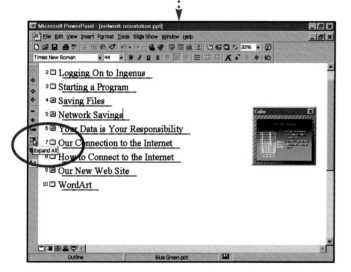

5 PowerPoint hides all the slides' details and underlines the titles of all the slides to show that they have hidden details. To display the hidden details, click on the **Expand All** button on the Outline toolbar. ■

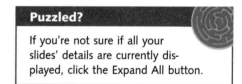

Puzzled?

If you're not sure if all your slides' details are currently displayed, click the Expand All button.

Rearranging Data in Outline View

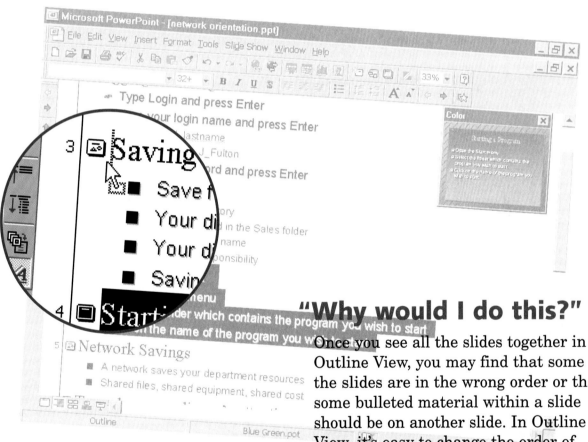

"Why would I do this?"

Once you see all the slides together in Outline View, you may find that some of the slides are in the wrong order or that some bulleted material within a slide should be on another slide. In Outline View, it's easy to change the order of slide text. You can move text up or down and indent it more or less than it already is. You can also change the location of a slide or slide text using the drag-and-drop method or the buttons on the Outline toolbar.

1 To move a slide in the outline, select it by clicking on its icon with the four-headed arrow pointer.

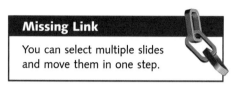

Missing Link

You can select multiple slides and move them in one step.

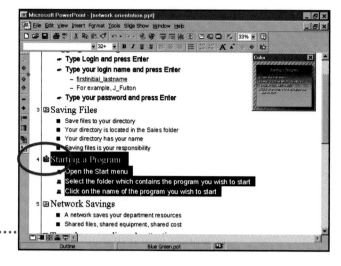

2 Click on the selected text and drag it to its new location. A horizontal line indicates the new location. When you release the mouse button, PowerPoint moves the slide to the new location and automatically renumbers all the slides accordingly.

Puzzled?

The number of a slide represents its order in your presentation, and it appears in front of the slide icon.

3 To move a bulleted text line on a slide, select the text with the four-headed arrow pointer by clicking the bulleted line's icon.

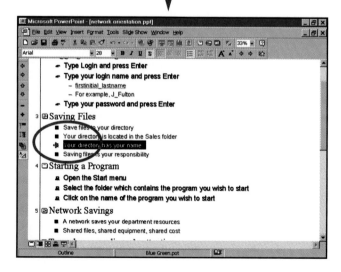

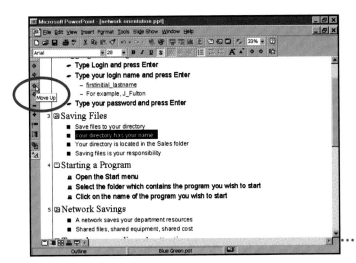

4 To move the text upward in the outline, click the **Move Up** button on the Outline toolbar. The selected text moves up one line. Repeat this as many times as necessary.

5 To move the slide text downward in the outline, click the **Move Down** button on the Outline toolbar as many times as necessary. The selected line moves down one line each time you click the Move Down button.

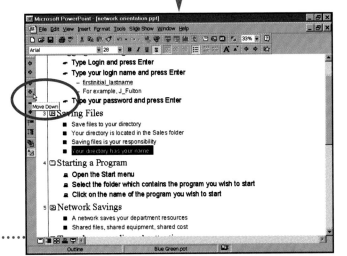

6 To move slide text to a higher level in the outline (to make a bulleted item a separate slide, for example), click the **Promote** button on the Outline toolbar. To move slide text to a lower level, click the **Demote** button on the Outline toolbar. ■

Missing Link

By experimenting with the Promote and Demote buttons, you can see if a new slide "works" as its own slide, or in a different position in the outline.

191

PART VIII

Creating Notes and Handouts

YOU CAN'T OVERESTIMATE THE IMPORTANCE of your presentation. However, the printed materials you pass out to your audience are of equal importance. If you've ever attended a presentation and wished you had a handout that would help you follow the discussion and on which you could take your own notes, you understand the importance of the tasks in this part.

With PowerPoint, you can print notes (called Speaker's Notes) to help you get through a presentation, and you can create audience handouts to help your audience follow it. An audience handout can include whatever you want: the contents of up to six slides, an outline, notes you've created, a combination of up to three slides and notes you've created, or a combination of up to three slides and blank lines on which the members of your audience can take their own notes. You can even print all of these handouts if you want! Of course, you don't want to inundate your audience with papers, but with the variety of printed material you can produce, you're bound to find something your audience would find helpful.

From another perspective, have you ever wished you could take notes while *giving* a presentation? Wouldn't it be great if you could take your own notes, record official meeting minutes yourself, or create a list of action items (things you personally need to act on when the presentation is over)? Well, PowerPoint contains a powerful tool called the Meeting Minder that enables you to keep a record about your presentation so you can create notes for follow-up after the presentation is over. As long as you have some sort of computer handy—whether it's a notebook or a desktop PC—you can use the Meeting Minder to create useful notes for yourself during the presentation.

You can create Notes, Meeting Minutes, and Action Items for every slide in your presentation. You can create the Notes either in the Notes Pages View or using the Meeting Minder—your choice! And regardless of whether you create your notes in Notes Page View or the Meeting Minder, you can edit them using either feature. Meeting Minutes tend to be more formal in tone than Notes. Whereas Notes can be humorous observations or reminders of topics you want to discuss, Meeting Minutes are generally observations you record about the slide you're discussing. Action Items are topics that you want to act on at a later time. For example, if a member of your audience asks you for statistical figures to back up a statement in a slide, you can create an Action Item reminding you to send those figures to the person who requested them.

At the conclusion of the presentation, the Meeting Minder creates a summary of its contents using Microsoft Word. You can save and print that summary, as well as a slide containing any Action Items you've created.

In this part, you'll see the range of printed materials you can create with PowerPoint. And you'll learn how you can help yourself and your audience get the most out of a presentation.

In order to use some of these features, such as the handouts and Meeting Minder, you must have Microsoft Word for Windows. Without Word, you can't get the most out of these features.

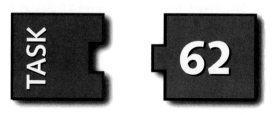

Creating Speaker's Notes

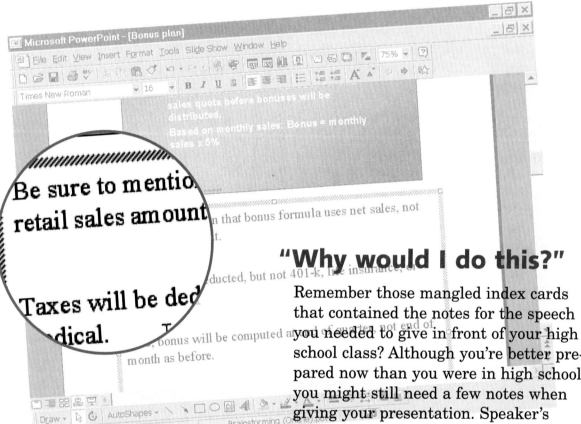

"Why would I do this?"

Remember those mangled index cards that contained the notes for the speech you needed to give in front of your high school class? Although you're better prepared now than you were in high school, you might still need a few notes when giving your presentation. Speaker's Notes are printouts on which you can include the contents of one or more slides as well as notes for particular slides (which you type directly in the presentation). You can use Speaker's Notes to remind you of important points you want to make or people you want to acknowledge, or for any other notes you want to make to yourself— notes do not appear in the on-screen presentation.

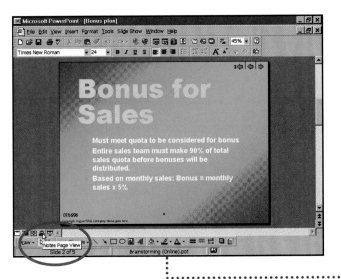

1 From any view, select a slide (or the text in a slide) that you want to make into Speaker's Notes. Then click the **Notes Page View** button.

Missing Link

In Notes Page View, the contents of the slide appears at the top of the window, and your notes will appear at the bottom.

2 The Notes Page View for the selected slide opens. You will enter your notes on the lower half of the page. If the page is too small for you to see the text clearly, click the **Zoom** drop-down arrow on the Standard toolbar and select a size that is easier to read.

Puzzled?

Setting the Zoom to 66% usually does the trick. However, if you still can't read the text, try a higher percentage.

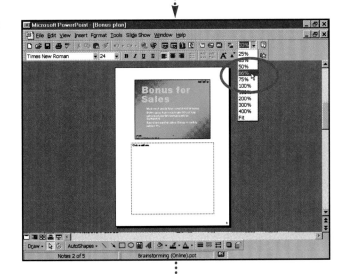

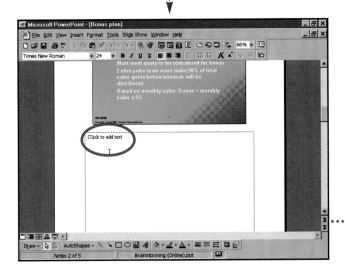

3 Click the **Click to add text** text box on the lower part of the page.

4 The words, "Click to add text," disappear, and a hatched border and blinking insertion point appear. This means that the area is selected and PowerPoint is ready for your notes.

Missing Link

By default, each page of Speaker's Notes contains one slide with the notes printed beneath it. In Task 64, you learn to print the Speaker's Notes in other styles to use as handouts.

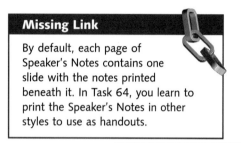

5 Type the text for your Speaker's Notes. You can select, edit, and drag and drop text just as you would the text in any PowerPoint slide.

Puzzled?

You can also add, delete, or edit existing Speaker's Notes. Just click on the Notes Page View button when the slide you want is active.

6 To add notes to another slide, click the **Next Slide** or the **Previous Slide** button. When you're through adding notes, simply select a different view, such as Slide View, by clicking the appropriate view button. PowerPoint saves your notes in the PowerPoint file; you do not have to perform additional steps to save them. ■

Puzzled?

You can print just your notes by opening the **File** menu and selecting **Print**, then selecting **Notes Pages** from the **Print what** list, and clicking **OK**.

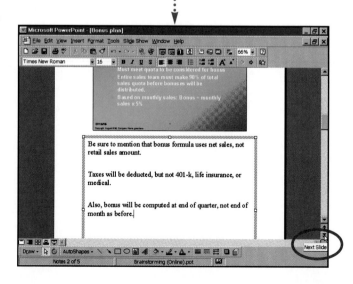

Creating Handouts

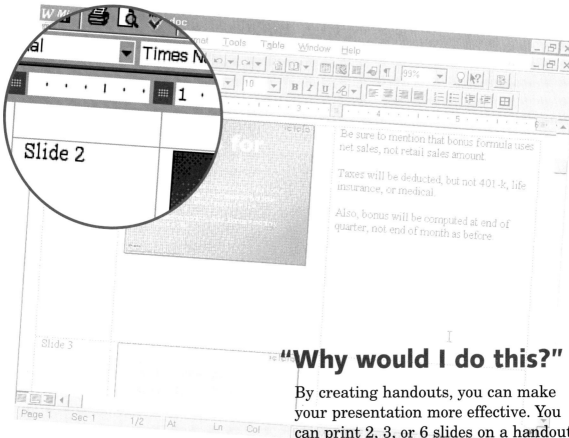

"Why would I do this?"

By creating handouts, you can make your presentation more effective. You can print 2, 3, or 6 slides on a handout page—whatever you want. And if you have Microsoft Word installed, you can create handouts that contain miniature versions of your slides, your Speaker's Notes, blank lines in which viewers can make their own notes, or a combination of any of these. You can also print an outline of your presentation.

1 From any view, open the **View** menu, select **Master**, and select **Handout Master**.

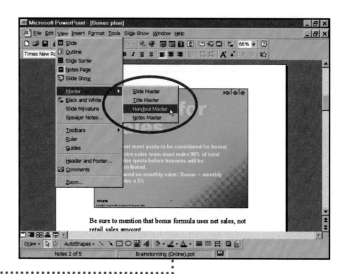

Missing Link

You create the look of your handouts with the Handout Master. The elements that you place on this master will appear on each handout.

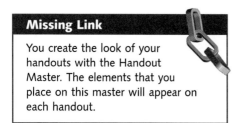

2 To add a header (which will print at the top of each handout), move the cursor over the word <header> and click. The cursor should appear in the text box—if it does not, then right-click the **Header Area** and select **Edit Text**. Then type your text.

Puzzled?

You can place a graphic (such as a company logo) in the header area with the **Insert**, **Picture** command.

3 To add a date to your handouts, click the words <date/time> in the Date Area. The cursor should appear in the text box. If it does not, right-click on the Date Area and select Edit Text from the pop-up menu. Then open the **Insert** menu and select **Date and Time**. The Date and Time dialog box appears.

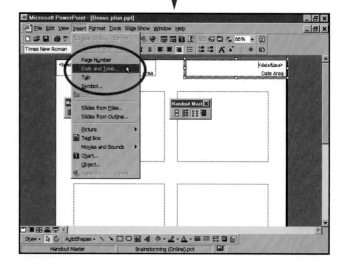

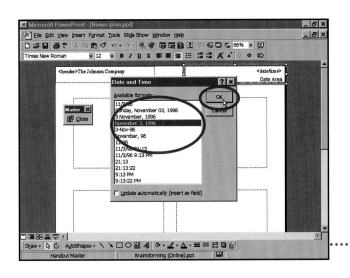

4 Select a date format and click **OK**. If you select the **Update automatically** checkbox, the date is inserted as a *field*, which means that it's automatically updated whenever you save your PowerPoint file.

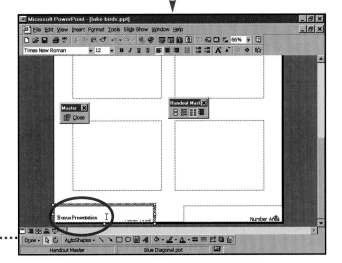

5 To add a footer (which will print at the bottom of every handout), click in the **Footer Area** and type your text. Again, you can add a graphic here with the **Insert, Picture** command. If the cursor does not appear in the Footer Area when you click it, then right-click on it and select **Edit Text** from the pop-up menu.

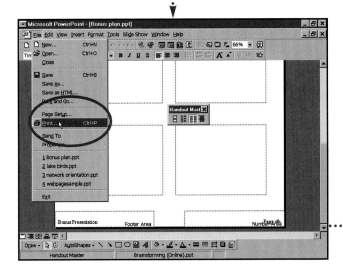

Missing Link

The # symbol that appears in the Number Area is the page number, which will print on each handout. You can click in the Number Area and add text, such as **Page**, so it will print as Page 1, Page 2, etc. You can delete the # symbol if you don't want the page number to appear.

6 When you're ready to print your handouts, open the **File** menu and select **Print**. The Print dialog box appears.

Task 63: Creating Handouts

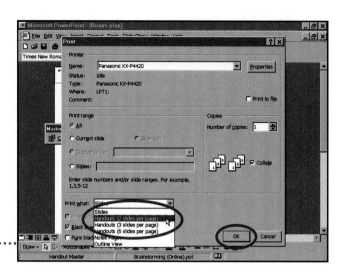

7 Open the **Print what** list box and select a handout option, such as **Handouts (2 slides per page)**. Click **OK** to print your handouts.

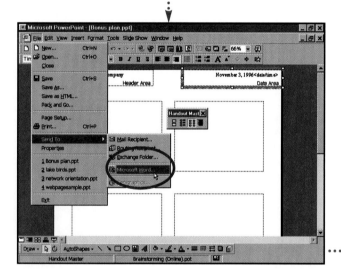

8 If you'd like to include your speaker's notes with the handouts, or if you'd like to leave space for your listeners to add their own notes, open the **File** menu, select **Send To**, and select **Microsoft Word**. (You must have the Microsoft Word program installed to perform steps 8 to 11.)

9 Select from the different configurations in the Write-Up dialog box, and click **OK**. For example, select **Notes next to slides**.

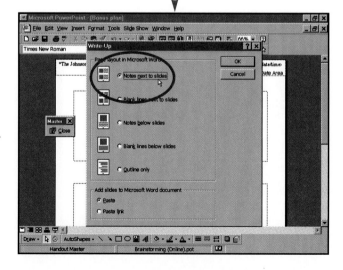

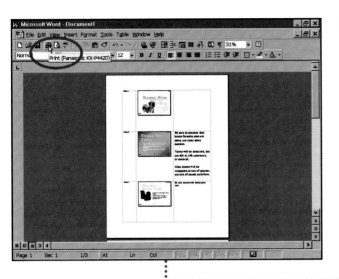

10 Microsoft Word opens a new document and places a thumbnail of each slide on as many pages as necessary. These pages reflect the choice you made in the Write-Up dialog box. To print your handouts, click the **Print** button on the Standard toolbar.

Puzzled?

If you haven't typed any notes, Word displays a blank space next to the slide.

11 When you're ready to return to PowerPoint, open the **File** menu and select **Exit**. Word will ask you if you'd like to save your handouts in a file. Click **Yes** if you do or **No** if you don't.

Missing Link

If you save your handouts in a file, you can view them or reprint them again if needed.

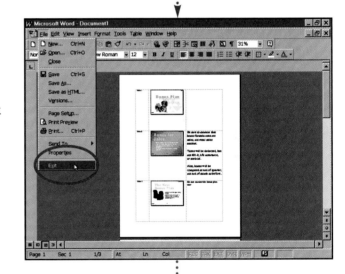

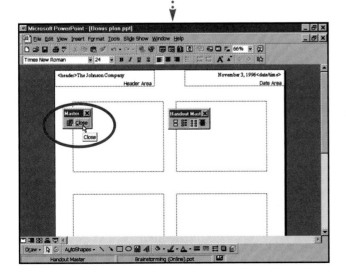

12 When you're through creating your handouts, click **Close** to return to a normal view. ■

Using the Meeting Minder

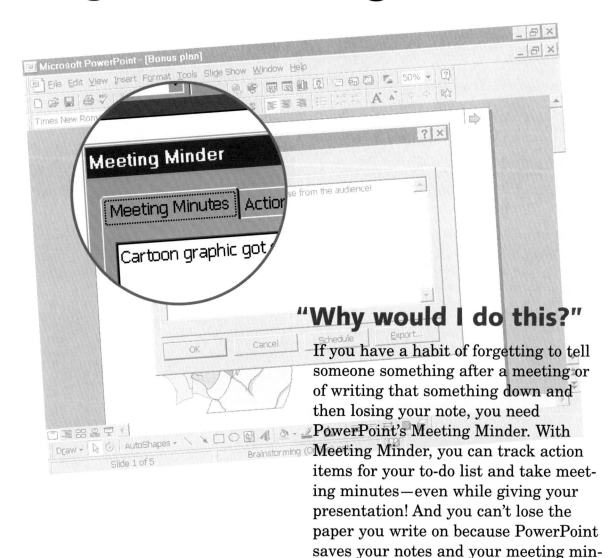

"Why would I do this?"

If you have a habit of forgetting to tell someone something after a meeting or of writing that something down and then losing your note, you need PowerPoint's Meeting Minder. With Meeting Minder, you can track action items for your to-do list and take meeting minutes—even while giving your presentation! And you can't lose the paper you write on because PowerPoint saves your notes and your meeting minutes with your presentation, which you can view again when needed. If you have Microsoft Word installed, you can print out your minutes and action items so you can give them to the appropriate persons.

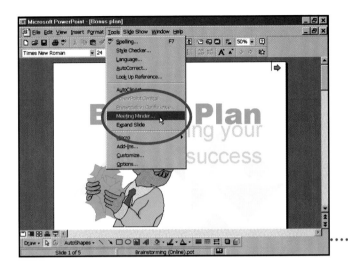

1 From any PowerPoint view, select the slide you want to comment on, open the **Tools** menu, and choose **Meeting Minder**.

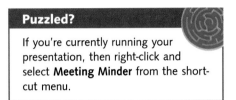

Puzzled?

If you're currently running your presentation, then right-click and select **Meeting Minder** from the short-cut menu.

2 The Meeting Minder dialog box contains tabs for Meeting Minutes and Action Items. To add a note to the minutes, click in the text area and begin typing. To add an action item, click the **Action Items** tab.

Missing Link

You can view your meeting minutes at a later time by choosing the **Tools, Meeting Minder** command again.

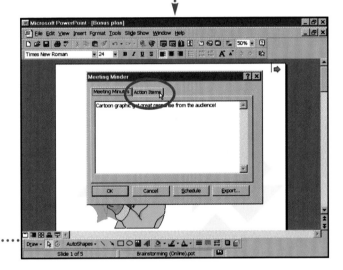

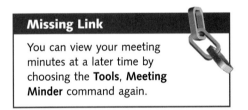

3 Click in the **Description** text area and type in your item. In the **Assigned To** area, type the name of the person to which this task is being assigned. Change the **Due Date** if needed, then click **Add** to add the item. Repeat to add more action items. Your action items appear at the end of your presentation on a new slide. When you're done adding action items, click **OK**.

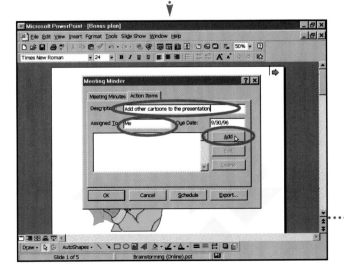

4 If you'd like to print your minutes and your action items, *and you have Microsoft Word installed*, then click **Export** in the Meeting Minder dialog box.

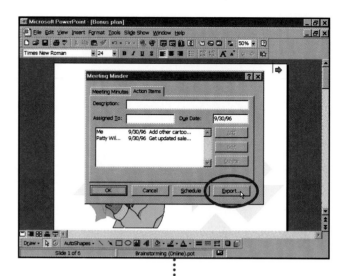

Puzzled?

If you've already closed the Meeting Minder dialog box, use the **Tools**, **Meeting Minder** command again to reopen it.

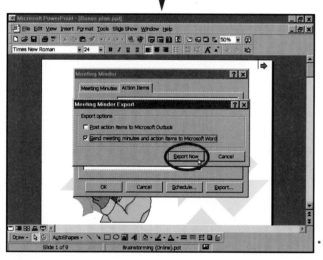

5 Click the **Send Meeting Minutes and Action Items to Microsoft Word** checkbox. Then click the **Export Now** button. Word opens a new document and adds your minutes and action items.

6 Click the **Print** button on the Standard toolbar to print the Word document that contains the meeting minutes and action items. ■

Missing Link

To return to PowerPoint, open the **File** menu and select **Exit**. Word will ask you if you'd like to save the meeting minutes and action items in a separate file for later viewing. Click **Yes** if you do or **No** if you don't.

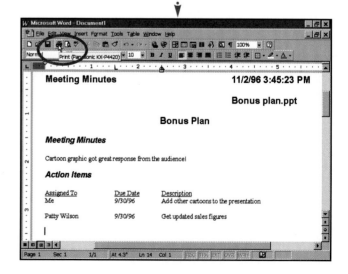

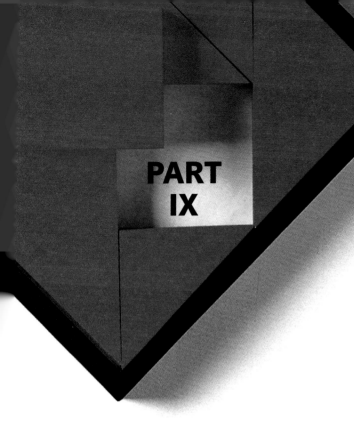

Part IX: Showing a Presentation

EVEN WHEN YOU THINK YOU'RE FINISHED with your slides, you'll still find things that need fixing. Although you can move your slides using the Outline View, you can also change the order of slides using the thumbnails that appear in the Slide Sorter View. (A *thumbnail* is a tiny representation of a slide; because they're small, PowerPoint can display more than one slide at a time.)

Once you've created your slides and added text, artwork, and all the other graphics you need, it's time to turn those slides into a slide show. A slide show consists of all the slides in the presentation you've worked so hard on, along with special effects which minimize the transition between the slides.

Each of these special effects (animation effects, sound effects, and transitions) adds a different look to your presentation. *Text animations* make each bulleted line of text appear independently. This feature is very effective if you want to focus your audience's attention on each item as you discuss it. In a text animation, you can choose from a variety of text effects: text can appear from many directions, and it can appear to become dim or a different color when the next line of text appears.

Within a slide show, your slides can contain the following special effects:

Special Effect	Description
Text animations	Controls how text appears on-screen
Graphic animations	Controls when graphics appear
Chart animations	Controls when each part of the chart appears
Sound effects	You can add sound to the particular chart element you animate
Transitions	Controls how each slide advances to the next

Graphic animations, like text and chart animations, can be accompanied by a sound effect. For example, one animation effect is the "Camera effect," which makes a sound like a clicking camera shutter while the selected object appears from its center to its outside edge. Of course, your computer needs to be capable of producing sounds in order for these animation effects to work correctly.

A *chart effect* allows you to control how your chart appears on-screen. For example, you can make each element (such as each series or each category) appear one after the other. This allows you to emphasize the different elements of a complex chart. A *transition effect* appears on-screen when your show advances from one slide to the next. PowerPoint offers 11 basic types of transitions. Because you can apply each of these transitions in different directions (for example, from the bottom of the slide, the top, the left, or the right), you have a total of 45 transitions to choose from.

Once you perfect your slides and add the appropriate special effects, you're ready to present them. PowerPoint provides you with a number of ways to display your presentation slides. In addition to being able to produce printed materials, you can print your slides on transparencies and display them on an overhead projector. This is not a very "hi-tech" method, but it is reasonably priced and available to most businesses.

In this part of the book, you learn how to start a slide show and run it manually and automatically. You also learn how to add special effects and graphics to your slides.

65

Changing the Order of Slides

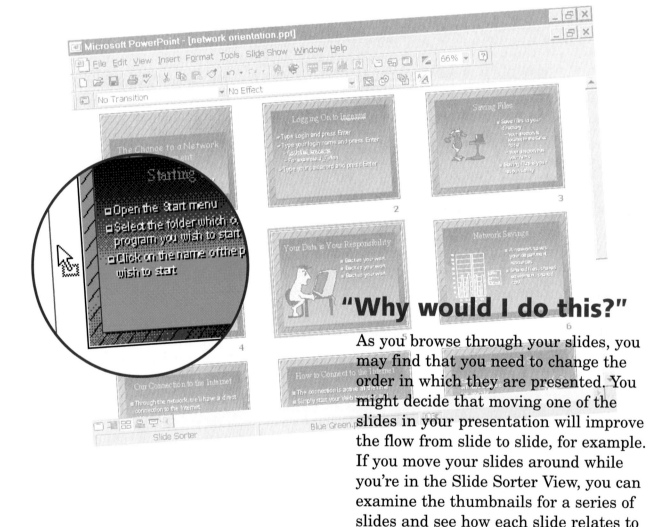

"Why would I do this?"

As you browse through your slides, you may find that you need to change the order in which they are presented. You might decide that moving one of the slides in your presentation will improve the flow from slide to slide, for example. If you move your slides around while you're in the Slide Sorter View, you can examine the thumbnails for a series of slides and see how each slide relates to the one before it and the one after it.

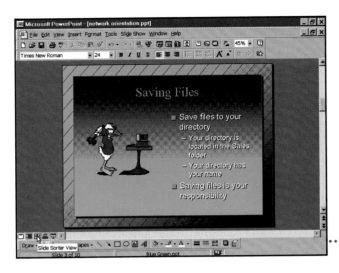

1 From any other view, click the **Slide Sorter View** button to switch to the Slide Sorter view.

2 If the slide you want to move does not have a dark border around it (indicating that it's selected), click it. Once you select it, a dark border appears around the slide.

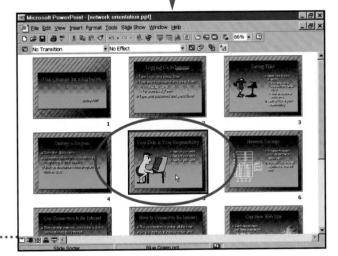

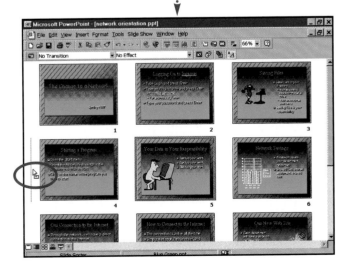

3 Click the selected slide, hold down the mouse button, and drag the slide to its new location. The drag-and-drop mouse pointer appears, and a vertical line marks the slide's new location. When you're satisfied with the slide's new location, release the mouse button. ■

Puzzled?

If you drag a slide to the wrong location or lift up the mouse button too early, click the **Undo** button on the Standard toolbar to reverse the action.

213

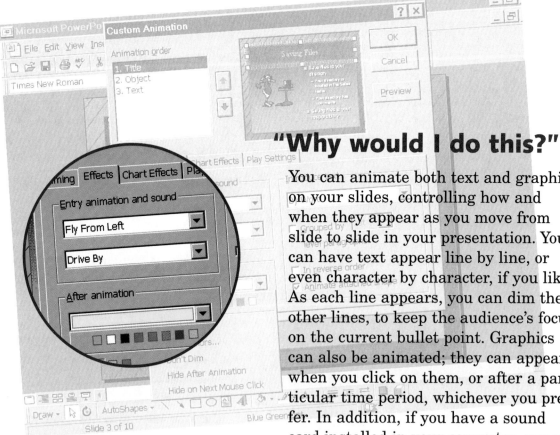

Adding Animation to Text and Graphics

"Why would I do this?"

You can animate both text and graphics on your slides, controlling how and when they appear as you move from slide to slide in your presentation. You can have text appear line by line, or even character by character, if you like. As each line appears, you can dim the other lines, to keep the audience's focus on the current bullet point. Graphics can also be animated; they can appear when you click on them, or after a particular time period, whichever you prefer. In addition, if you have a sound card installed in your computer, you will find that most of the animation effects have accompanying sound effects. For example, the Camera Effect makes a sound like a camera shutter. Use animation effects to set your presentation apart from all the rest.

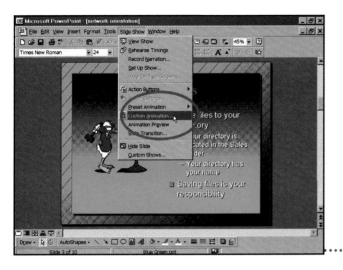

1 From the Slide View, switch to the slide to which you want to add animation. Then open the **Slide Show** menu and select **Custom Animation**.

Missing Link

To quickly animate an item on a slide, click on that item, then open the **Slide Show** menu. Select an option off the **Preset Animation** submenu. (You need to be in Slide View to do this.)

2 You can animate the title, text, and/or graphics on your slide. Click on the *first* item you wish to animate in the **Slide objects without animation** list. Then click the **Animate** option from the Start animation panel. Normally, items are animated when you click them during your presentation, but you can animate them automatically by selecting that option and the number of seconds you want Power-Point to wait before starting.

3 Click the **Effects** tab. Select an item from the **Animation order** list, then select animation and/or sound options you want. If you want a line of text to change color or become dim when the next line appears, click the **After animation** drop-down list arrow and select a new color. You can use the **Don't Dim** option to make sure text does not dim, or use one of the **Hide** options to make the text appear to vanish when the next line of text appears. Then click **Previous** to view your animation.

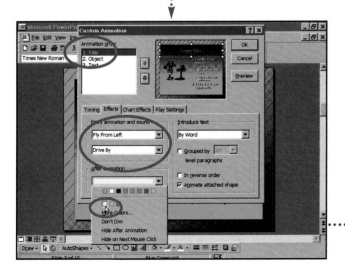

Task 66: Adding Animation to Text and Graphics

4 If the item you selected in step three was the title or the text, then you can animate it by selecting an option from the **Introduce text** list. You can even make the text appear in reverse by selecting the **In reverse order** option. Repeat steps 3 and 4 for additional animation items.

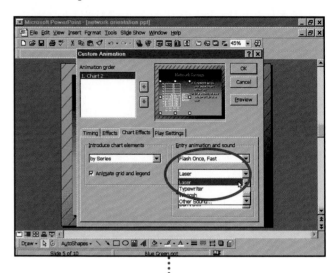

Missing Link

Text is normally animated one bulleted item at a time, but you can animate sub-bullets (indented items) separately by selecting 2nd, etc. from the **Grouped by** list.

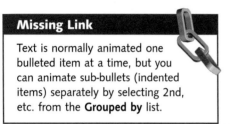

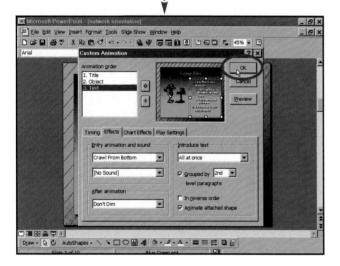

5 After you make all your choices, click **OK**. If you want to animate another slide, change to it and then repeat these steps. ■

Puzzled?

You can preview your presentation (complete with animations) by clicking the **Slide Show View** button (the fifth button from the left just above the PowerPoint status bar). PowerPoint starts the slide show from the active slide. Click the mouse button to advance through the presentation.

Adding Animation to Charts

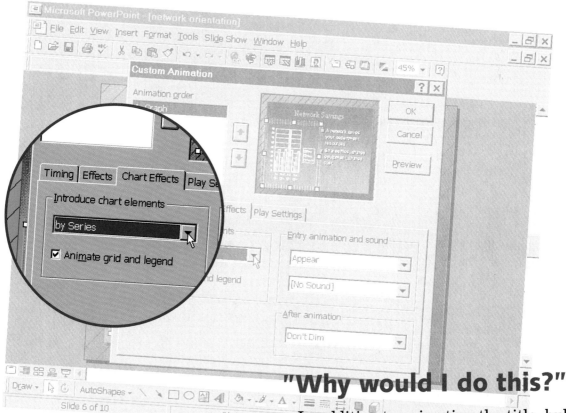

"Why would I do this?"

In addition to animating the title, bulleted text, or graphics on a slide, you can also animate your charts. You can animate the chart itself, or each series or category. If you like, you can even add sound to herald the chart's appearance on the slide. Animating a chart draws importance to it, focusing your audience's attention on an important element of your slide.

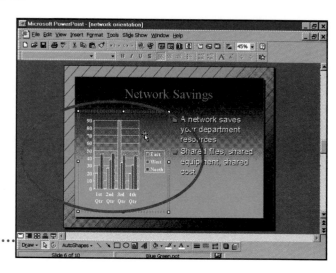

1 In Slide View, click the chart you wish to animate. Handles (small white boxes) appear around the chart to show that it's selected.

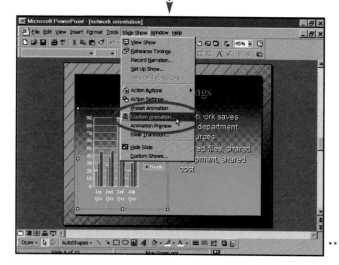

2 Open the **Slide Show** menu and select **Custom Animation**. The Custom Animation dialog box appears, open to the **Chart Effects** tab.

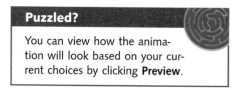

Puzzled?

You can view how the animation will look based on your current choices by clicking **Preview**.

3 Select how you want to animate the chart by selecting an option from the **Introduce chart elements** list. For example, the **All at once** option makes all of the chart elements appear at one time. The **by Series** option, on the other hand, makes the chart elements appear by series. You can have the grid and the legend appear at the same time as the chart by selecting **Animate grid and legend**.

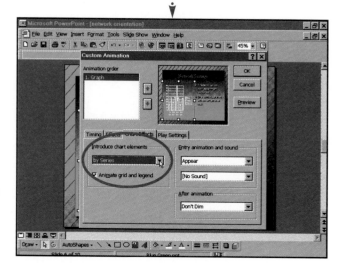

218

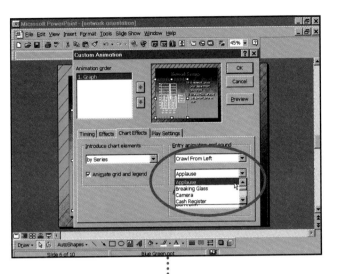

4 Under **Entry animation and sound**, you can choose the manner in which you want the chart elements to appear (such as Flash Once, Fast), and whether or not you want the animation accompanied by some sound.

> **Puzzled?**
>
> If you're looking for one of the Fly effects (such as Fly From Right), they are only available if you select **All at once** from the Introduce chart elements list.

5 If you want the chart elements (or the chart itself, if that's what you choose in step 3) to change color or become dim after it appears, click the **After animation** drop-down list arrow and select a color—the colors in your list may be different from the ones shown here; what you see depends on the color choices you've made previously. (Choose one of the **Hide** options to make the item appear to vanish soon after it appears.)

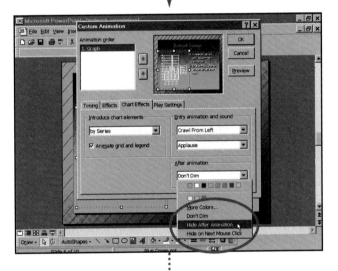

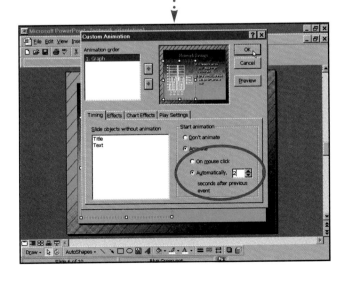

6 If you want the chart to appear automatically when you display that slide during your presentation, click the **Timing** tab and select **Automatically**, and set the number of seconds you want PowerPoint to wait before displaying the chart. When you're through selecting options, click **OK**. ■

Adding Transitions Between Slides

"Why would I do this?"

Special effects make your presentation sparkle, and the way in which one slide advances to the next can add drama to your slides and make you look like a star! You can apply transition effects to make one slide progress smoothly to the next. You can also use certain transitions to "announce" to your viewers that something new is coming up.

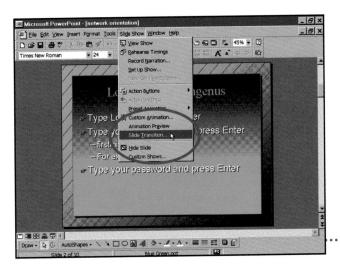

1 Select the slide you want to work with in Slide View. Then open the **Slide Show** and choose **Slide Transition**. The Slide Transition dialog box appears.

2 Select a transition effect from the **Effect** drop-down list.

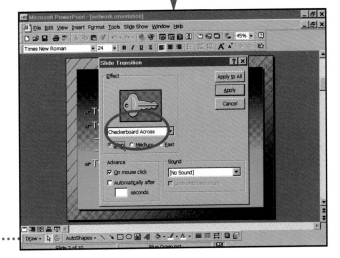

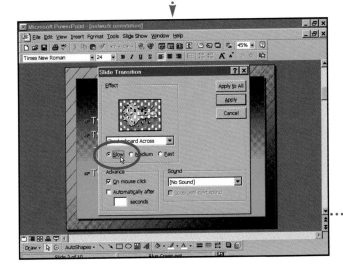

3 Choose the speed of the transition by clicking the **Slow**, **Medium**, or **Fast** option.

Missing Link

To see the effect another time, click the speed option again. For example, click **Medium**.

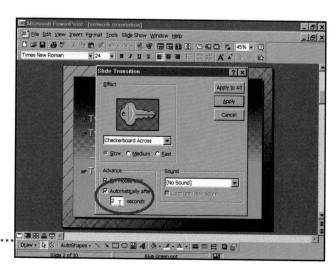

4 The Advance options enable you to control whether the slides advance automatically or only when you click the mouse. If you choose to have PowerPoint change them automatically, indicate the number of seconds you want the slide to remain on-screen. (Task 72 shows you how to set and rehearse custom timing options.)

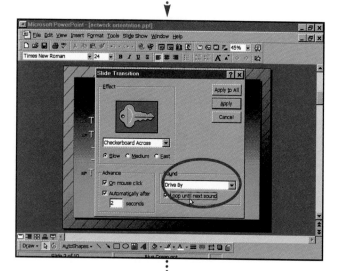

5 Click the **Sound** drop-down list arrow and choose a sound effect to go with the transition. You can set different sounds for different slides (as appropriate for the context of each slide) or no sound at all. In addition, you can have your sound repeat (loop) until the next sound in your presentation.

> **Puzzled?**
>
> If the sound effect you select doesn't work, your computer may not be capable of producing sounds.

6 When you're satisfied with the transition effect for the selected slide, click **Apply**. If you want to apply this same transition to all the slides in your presentation, click **Apply to All** instead. If you choose Apply, you can repeat these steps for the other slides in your presentation to which you want to apply a transition effect. ■

> **Puzzled?**
>
> If you decide you don't like a transition you've applied, you can change it by repeating these steps.

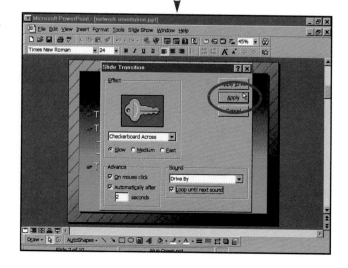

Adding Sounds and Video Clips

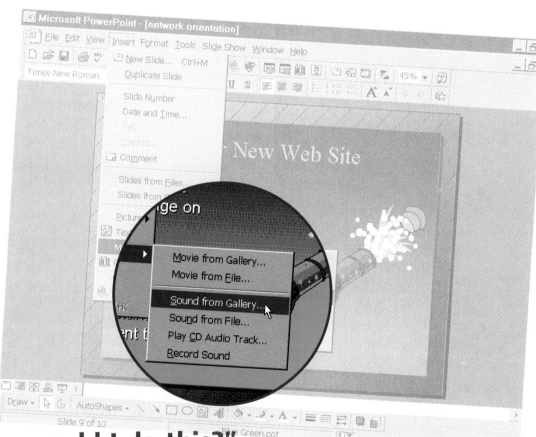

"Why would I do this?"

They say that a picture is worth a thousand words. So a moving picture must be worth about ten thousand words. If you want to add real pizzazz to your presentation, incorporate sound or video clips on your slides. PowerPoint comes with a Gallery of sounds and video

clips, or you can add your own. If your PC has a CD-ROM, you can incorporate a sound from it. In addition, you can even record your own sounds and incorporate them into your presentation.

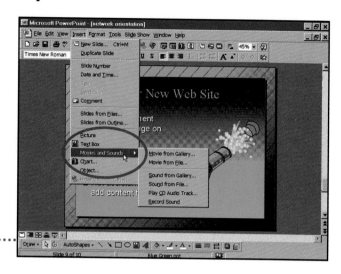

1 In Slide View, select the slide you wish to work with. Then open the **Insert** menu and select **Movies and Sounds**. A sub-menu appears.

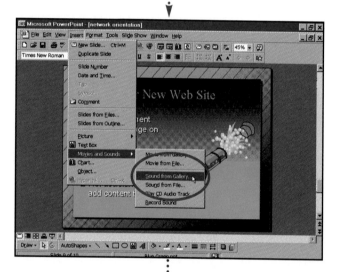

2 Select the option you want off the sub-menu. For example, select **Sound from Gallery**.

Puzzled?

You may see a message telling you to insert the PowerPoint CD-ROM in order for you to add more clips to the Gallery. If you have the CD-ROM and you'd like to add more clips, then insert it before you click **OK**. The clips are automatically added to the Gallery.

3 If you selected Sound or Movie from Gallery, the Microsoft Clip Gallery dialog box appears. Click an icon to select that particular movie or sound, then click **Insert** to insert it. An icon, representing the clip, appears on the slide. To play the clip, double-click its icon.

Puzzled?

You can download sound and movie files from Microsoft's Web site. Connect to the Internet in the usual manner, then click the **Connect to Web for additional clips** icon (the globe).

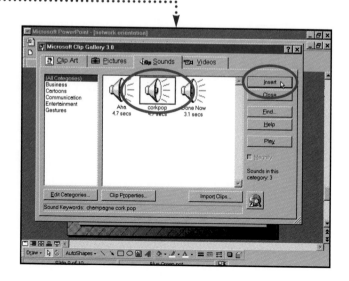

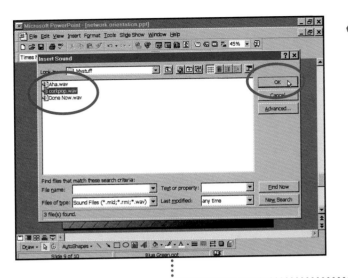

4 If you selected **Sound from File** or **Movie from File** in step 2, then a file dialog box like this appears. Change to the folder that contains your file, select it, then click **OK** to insert it. An appropriate icon (such as a horn or a projector) appears on the slide to indicate the inserted file.

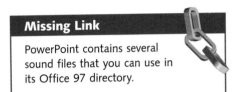

Missing Link

PowerPoint contains several sound files that you can use in its Office 97 directory.

5 If you selected **Play CD Audio Track** in step 2, the Play Options dialog box appears. Select the track number, start time, and stop time of the sound you want to use. Click **OK** to insert the sound clip. A CD-ROM icon appears on the slide.

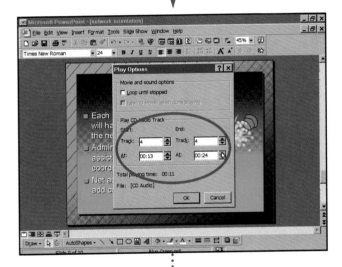

Missing Link

You don't need to insert the CD that contains your sound in order to complete step 5.

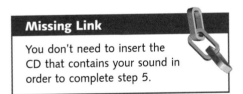

6 If your PC is equipped with a microphone, then you can record your own sound and incorporate it on a slide. Turn your micro-phone on and then select **Record Sound** in step 2. Type a **Name** for the sound, then click the **Record** button (the circle). Record your sound and when you're through, click the **Stop** button (the square). ■

Hiding a Slide

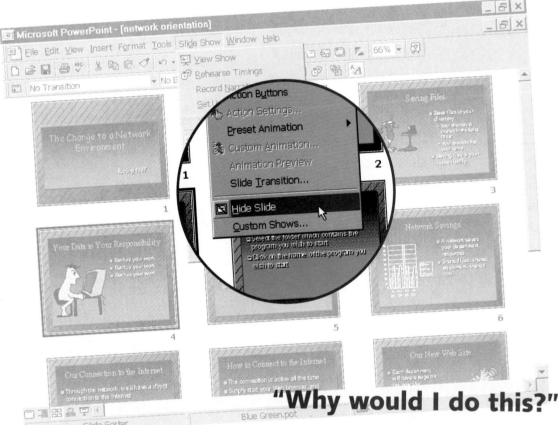

"Why would I do this?"

You can hide a slide if you anticipate that you might not want to show it during your presentation. By hiding a slide, you provide yourself the option of skipping over it if it doesn't seem appropriate for a particular presentation. It also means that you can create slides for different situations and then decide on the spot whether to show or skip those slides.

1 Switch to the slide you wish to hide, then click the **Slide Sorter View** button.

Missing Link

To view a hidden slide during a slide show, press **H**. Task 73 covers techniques you can use to move between slides.

2 Select the slide you want to hide by clicking it. A dark border surrounds the slide you select. Open the **Slide Show** menu and choose **Hide Slide**. The Hide Slide command toggles between hiding and not hiding a slide; click the command once to turn it on and again to turn it off. When a slide is hidden, the Hide Slide icon appears depressed on the menu.

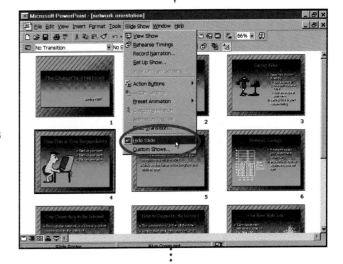

Puzzled?

If you accidentally tell PowerPoint to hide a slide, open the **Slide Show** menu and choose **Hide Slide** again to turn the option off.

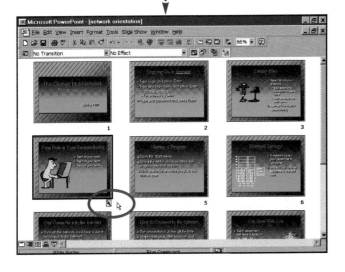

3 In the Slide Sorter View, PowerPoint displays a slash through the slide number of the hidden slide. ∎

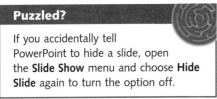

TASK

71

Adding Timing to Slides

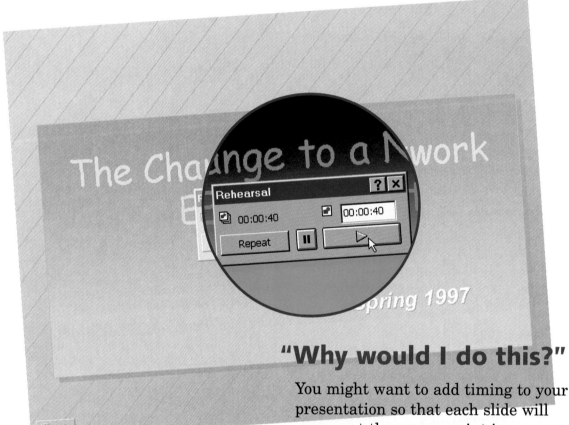

"Why would I do this?"

You might want to add timing to your presentation so that each slide will appear at the proper point in your verbal commentary. By adding timing, you can run your presentation unattended or with minimal effort. Or, you might add timing to your slides to vary the length of time between text transitions, for example, or to make slides with a lot of information remain on-screen longer. When you add timing to your slides, PowerPoint displays the amount of time for each slide under the slide's thumbnail in the Slide Sorter View.

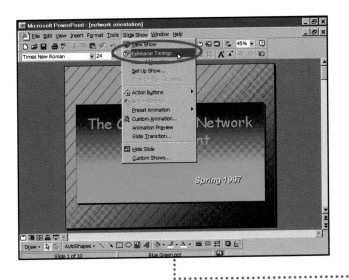

1 From any view, open the **Slide Show** menu and choose **Rehearse Timings**. (If you're in Slide Sorter view, you can click the **Rehearse Timings** button on the Slide Sorter toolbar.) The screen goes blank as PowerPoint prepares to run your show.

> **Puzzled?**
>
> If you need to change the timing of your slides, you can repeat these steps.

2 The Rehearsal dialog box appears; it keeps track of how much time you spend on each slide. As you rehearse your lines verbally, use the VCR-like buttons in the dialog box to advance between slides. Click the **Play** button (the arrow) to advance to the next slide; click the **Pause** button (the two vertical bars) to temporarily stop the timer.

> **Puzzled?**
>
> If you make a mistake, click the **Repeat** button to start the timing over for that slide.

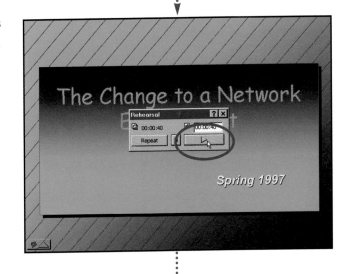

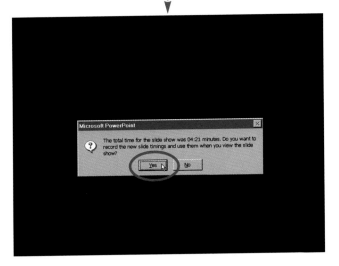

3 After you add timings to all the slides, PowerPoint shows you the total amount of time you need for the presentation. When PowerPoint asks you if you want to record the new slide timings, click **Yes**.

Task 71: Adding Timing to Slides

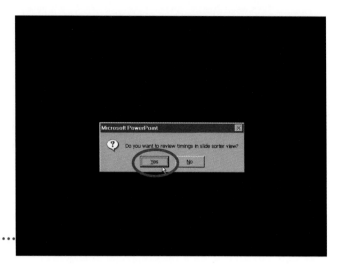

4 To review the timings for each slide, switch to Slide Sorter View by clicking **Yes**.

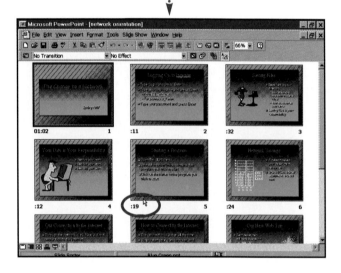

5 PowerPoint applies your new timings to the slides and returns you to the Slide Sorter View. Under each slide, you see the amount of time you allotted for it. ■

Running a Slide Show

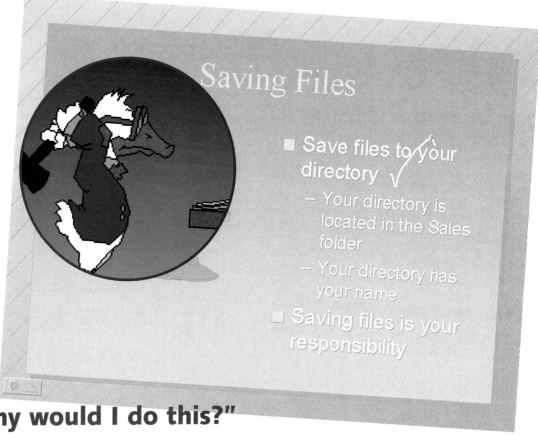

"Why would I do this?"

After you prepare, polish, and rehearse your presentation, your big day finally comes. It's time to show your presentation to the people for whom you prepared it. You can easily run the professional-quality slide show you've put together with a minimal amount of effort. And you can even write on your slides during the presentation to add emphasis to a particular point.

1 Before you start your show, select the options you want by opening the **Slide Show** menu and selecting **Set Up Show**.

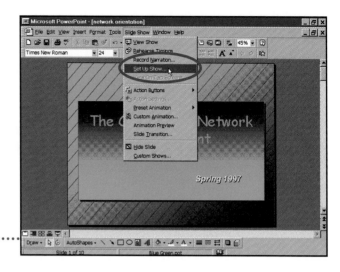

Missing Link

You might want to complete your setup before your audience arrives.

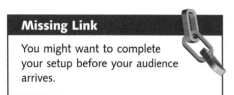

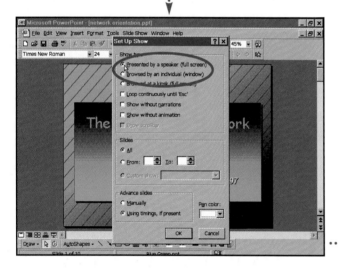

2 Under **Show type**, select how you want to present your PowerPoint show. If you're planning on presenting the show yourself, you might want it featured in a full screen. If the show is going to run unattended at a trade show, for example, you might want it to loop continuously.

3 Under **Slides**, select which slides you want to show. Normally, all of the slides are presented, but you can select a group of slides (such as numbers 7 to 15) to show instead.

Missing Link

During the show, you can use the Next, Previous, and Go commands on the shortcut menu (which appears when your right-click a slide) to jump to a specific slide during the show.

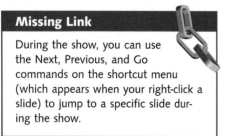

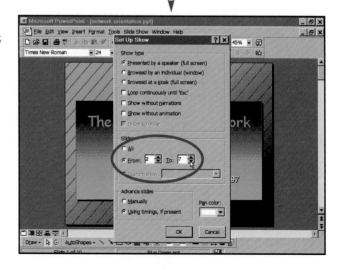

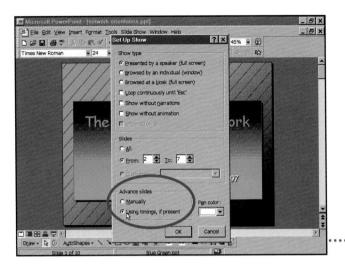

4 Under **Advance slides**, select how you want to handle the presentation. For example, if you select **Manually**, you must advance each slide by clicking the mouse button. If you choose **Using timings**, **if present**, then the slides advance automatically, based on the timings you created using Task 72.

5 As the presentation runs, you can add notes to the slides to emphasize points or to check off items you've finished discussing. To change the color of the pen, click the **Pen Color** drop-down list arrow and choose a new color. (Your color list may look different from the one shown here; the colors listed are colors you've selected previously.) When you're through setting up your presentation, click **OK**.

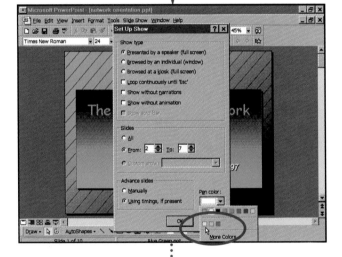

Puzzled?

Any marks you create on a slide are temporary; they disappear when you advance to the next slide.

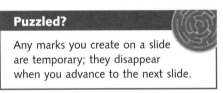

6 When you're ready to start the show, switch to your first slide, then click the **Slide Show** button. The screen goes blank as PowerPoint prepares to run your presentation.

Puzzled?

To go back to the previous slide during a slide show, press **P**. To display a hidden slide, press **H**. (If more than one slide is hidden, press H right before the first hidden slide comes up.)

7 At any time during the slide show, you can open a shortcut menu by clicking the button in the lower-left corner of the slide. From the shortcut menu, you can select from various commands. For example, select **Pen** to turn on the pen (or press Ctrl+P to avoid using the mouse or the shortcut menu).

Missing Link

The shortcut menu also gives you access to the Meeting Minder feature, that you can use to make notes to yourself.

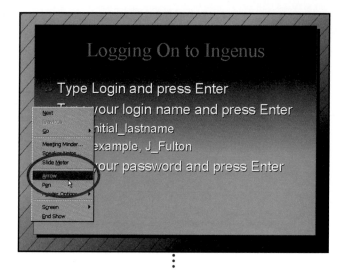

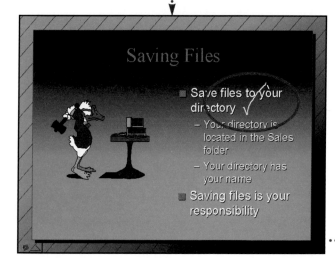

8 The mouse pointer turns into a pen. You can write on a slide by clicking and dragging the pen pointer to create shapes or characters. (The marks you make on a slide are not saved.)

9 When the slide show ends, you're returned to the PowerPoint screen, and your first slide is displayed. ■

Missing Link

To end your show with a black slide, before you start your presentation, open the **Tools** menu and select **Options**. Then select the **End with black slide** option and click **OK**.

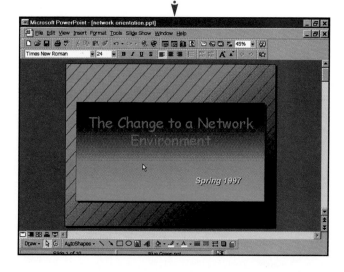

Reference

If you cannot remember how to access a particular PowerPoint feature, use this list to find the appropriate command and shortcut key.

Feature	Menu, Command	Shortcut Key
Action Items	Tools, Meeting Minder (Action Items tab)	(none)
Clip Art	Insert, Picture, Clip Art	(none)
Close File	File, Close	Ctrl+F4
Copy	Edit, Copy	Ctrl+C
Cut	Edit, Cut	Ctrl+X
Delete Slide	Edit, Delete Slide	(none)
Exit PowerPoint	File, Exit	Alt+F4
Find	Edit, Find	Ctrl+F
Font	Format, Font	(none)
Help	Microsoft PowerPoint Help	F1
Hide Slide	Slide Show, Hide Slide	(none)
Master Slide	View, Master, Slide Master	(none)
Meeting Minutes	Tools, Meeting Minder (Meeting Minutes tab)	(none)
Move	Edit, Cut and then Edit, Paste	Ctrl+X, then Ctrl+V
New File	File, New	Ctrl+N
New Slide	Insert, New Slide	Ctrl+M
Notes Pages	View, Notes Page	(none)
Object	Insert, Object	(none)
Open File	File, Open	Ctrl+O
Paste	Edit, Paste	Ctrl+V

Feature	Menu, Command	Shortcut Key
Print	File, Print	Ctrl+P
Redo	Edit, Redo	Ctrl+Y
Replace	Edit, Replace	Ctrl+H
Save As	File, Save As	(none)
Save	File, Save	Ctrl+S
Select All	Edit, Select All	Ctrl+A
Slide Layout	Format, Slide Layout	(none)
Slide Transition	Slide Show, Slide Transition	(none)
Spelling	Tools, Spelling	F7
Text Alignment	Format, Alignment	(none)
Undo	Edit, Undo	Ctrl+Z

Toolbar Guide

The following tables show the buttons on the most popular PowerPoint toolbars. To display a toolbar, use the View, Toolbars command.

Standard Toolbar

Button	Name	Description
	New	Creates a new presentation
	Open	Opens a presentation
	Save	Saves a presentation
	Print	Prints a presentation
	Spelling	Checks the spelling in a presentation
	Cut	Cuts the selected text or object from the slide and places it in the Clipboard
	Copy	Copies the selected text or object and places the copy in the Clipboard

Standard Toolbar

Button	Name	Description
	Paste	Pastes the contents of the Clipboard to the slide
	Format Painter	Copies the attributes of the selection
	Undo	Reverses the effect of the last operation
	Redo	Reverses the effect of Undo
	Insert Hyperlink	Inserts link to a Web document
	Web Toolbar	Displays the Web toolbar
	Insert Word Table	Inserts a table
	Insert Excel Worksheet	Inserts a worksheet
	Insert Chart	Inserts a chart
	Insert Clip Art	Opens the Microsoft ClipArt Gallery
	Insert New Slide	Inserts a new slide into the presentation
	Apply Design	Applies a different design template
	Black and White View	Changes slide colors to shades of gray
69%	Zoom	Makes images larger or smaller
	Office Assistant	Gives helpful information on a variety of topics

Formatting Toolbar

Button	Name	Description
Arial	Font	Changes the font of the selection
24	Font Size	Changes the font size of the selection (you specify the size)
B	Bold	Makes characters bold
I	Italic	Makes characters italic

Formatting Toolbar (continued)

Button	Name	Description
U	Underline	Makes characters underlined
S	Text Shadow	Adds a shadow to characters
	Left Alignment	Aligns text with the left margin
	Center Alignment	Aligns text between the two margins
	Right Alignment	Aligns text with the right margin
	Bullets	Turns on/off bullets in lists
	Increase Paragraph Spacing	Increases spaces between paragraphs
	Decrease Paragraph Spacing	Decreases spaces between paragraphs
A	Increase Font Size	Makes the font larger
A	Decrease Font Size	Makes the font smaller
	Promote (Indent less)	Makes text more important
	Demote (Indent more)	Makes text less important
	Animation Effects	Controls when graphics and text appear on a slide during a presentaion

Scroll Bar Buttons

Button	Name	Description
	Slide View	Displays only the selected slide
	Outline View	Displays slide text only—no graphics
	Slide Sorter View	Displays miniature versions of all the slides
	Notes Pages View	Displays a miniature slide above a text area in which you can type notes
	Slide Show	Shows the slides with all special effects

Drawing Toolbar

Button	Name	Description
Draw ▾	Draw	Provides access to additional drawing commands
	Select Objects	Selects a slide object or text box
	Free Rotate	Rotates an object
AutoShapes ▾	AutoShapes	Draws a variety of preformed shapes
	Line	Draws a straight line
	Arrow	Draws an arrow
	Rectangle	Draws a rectangle or square shape
	Oval	Draws a circle or oval shape
	Text Box	Inserts a text box
	WordArt	Twists and bends text
	Fill Color	Assigns a color to the interior of a shape
	Line Color	Assigns a color to an existing line
	Font Color	Assigns a color to existing text
	Line Style	Changes the weight of an existing line
	Dash Style	Changes the style of a dashed line
	Arrow Style	Changes the style of an arrowhead
	Shadow	Adds a shadow
	3-D	Adds a 3-dimensional effect

Outlining Toolbar

Button	Name	Description
	Promote (Indent less)	Makes text more important
	Demote (Indent more)	Makes text less important

Reference

Outlining Toolbar (continued)

Button	Name	Description
	Move Up	Moves a line upward in the outline
	Move Down	Moves a line downward in the outline
	Collapse Selection	Hides outline details in the active slide (usually the text within the slide)
	Expand Selection	Shows outline details in the active slide
	Collapse All	Hides outline details for all slides
	Expand All	Shows outline details for all slides
	Summary Slide	Creates a summary slide from titles of selected slides
	Show Formatting	Hides/Shows formatting attributes in the outline

Picture Toolbar

Button	Name	Description
	Insert Picture from file	Inserts a clip art from a file
	Image Control	Selects from preset color options
	More Contrast	Adds more contrast to graphic
	Less Contrast	Removes contrast from graphic
	More Brightness	Adds brightness to graphic
	Less Brightness	Removes brightness from graphic
	Crop	Hides part of graphic
	Line Style	Changes border style
	Recolor Picture	Changes the colors in graphic
	Format Drawing Object	Selects from various graphic options

Picture Toolbar

Button	Name	Description
	Set Transparent Color	Changes background
	Reset Picture	Resets graphic to original form

Animation Effects

Button	Name	Description
	Animate Title	Controls when title is displayed
	Animate Slide Text	Controls when text is displayed
	Drive-In	Adds drive-in effect
	Flying	Adds flying effect
	Camera	Adds camera effect
	Flash Once	Adds flash once effect
	Laser Text	Adds laser effect to text
	Typewriter	Adds typewriter effect to text
	Reverse Order	Adds reverse order effect
	Drop-In	Adds drop-in effect
	Animation Order	Changes order of the animation
	Custom Animation	Displays the Custom Animation dialog box

Appendix A

Installing and Using the IntelliPoint Mouse

If you purchased PowerPoint as part of the Microsoft Office 97 package, then you have a Microsoft IntelliPoint mouse (called IntelliMouse for short). Although similar in shape to the standard two-button Microsoft mouse, this mouse has a small gray wheel between the two buttons. That wheel gives you much more control over scrolling and entering commands.

To install the mouse, follow these steps:

1. Exit all applications.

2. Shut down Windows and turn off your computer.

3. Unplug your old mouse and plug in the new IntelliMouse.

4. Turn everything back on.

5. Insert the floppy disk that came with the mouse into your computer's floppy drive.

6. Click the **Start** button on the Windows taskbar.

7. Highlight **Settings** and, in the cascading menu that appears, choose **Control Panel**.

8. In the Control Panel window, double-click the **Add/Remove Programs** icon. You'll see the Add/Remove Programs Properties dialog box.

9. Click the **Install** button, and the Install Wizard displays a dialog box, telling you to insert the Microsoft Office CD or the first installation disk.

10. Insert the CD or disk, and then click **Next**. Windows searches the installation disk for the installation program. You'll see a dialog box suggesting the installation path, which you'll want to accept. The path shows the drive letter containing the installation program, followed by the title of the installation program. For example, if your floppy drive is A, you'll see an installation path of A:\SETUP.EXE.

11. Click **Finish**, and the installation program begins. During the installation process, you'll see dialog boxes asking for some basic information such as your name. Answer the questions as necessary by clicking the appropriate buttons.

Now you can start using the mouse. The left and right mouse buttons work as they always have, but in applications that support the IntelliMouse (including all of the Office 97 applications), you can do two things with the wheel: spin it and click it. What spinning and clicking do depends on the application you're in. In PowerPoint, you can use the wheel to take the following actions:

- **Scroll up or down a few rows at a time.** Rotate the wheel forward or backward.

- **Zoom in or out.** Hold down the **Ctrl** key and rotate the wheel. Rotate forward to zoom in; rotate backward to zoom out.

- **Expand or collapse information while in Outline view.** Point to a heading, then press and hold the **Shift** key as you rotate the wheel forward or backward.

> **Missing Link**
>
> If you find that you zoom more than you scroll, you can set the wheel button to zoom instead of scroll. Choose **Tools**, **Options**, and click the **General** tab. Click to place a check mark in the **Zoom on Roll with IntelliMouse** check box.

To view general Help on how to use the IntelliMouse, open the Windows **Start** menu and highlight **Programs**. Highlight **Microsoft Input Devices**, highlight **Mouse**, and click **IntelliPoint Online User's Guide**.

> **Missing Link**
>
> You can set the IntelliMouse options the same way you set your old mouse options in Windows 95. Display the **Control Panel** and double-click the **Mouse** icon. The Mouse Properties dialog box displays options that enable you to turn the wheel and wheel button on or off, among other options.

Glossary

3-D   Three-dimensional. You can add a "third dimension" to a graphic or a chart so that it looks as if it has depth.

Action Items   Items you want to remember and respond to by doing something. An example of an action item is "Follow up on this next week by asking Mr. Jones the results of his survey. Distribute the findings in the monthly memo to the Board of Directors." You can create action items during a presentation; you just jot down ideas as you think of them. The Meeting Minder compiles all action items into a new slide at the end of your presentation.

Animation Effects   A special transition that you can apply to a single object within a slide, such as the title, the bulleted text, or a graphic. Generally, these effects include sound.

attribute   A quality or characteristic you apply to text, charts, tables, and so on. An attribute of text might be its font or size; an attribute of a chart might be the color or line width of a feature.

AutoLayout   One of PowerPoint's predesigned slides to which you can add your own text. Each AutoLayout contains placeholders and formatting for items within the specific layout. Examples of AutoLayouts include a Title slide and Bulleted List slide.

bullet   A symbol such as a large dot, check mark, or small box that you place at the beginning of each item in a list. A bullet emphasizes the items in the list; each item in a bulleted list is equally important.

Bulleted List   One of PowerPoint's AutoLayouts; it is preformatted to include a list of equally important items.

cell   Area in a table or datasheet in which you enter data; the intersection of column and row.

chart   A visual representation of data you enter in a datasheet. Also known as a graph.

check box   An option you use to turn a feature on or off. When you click in a check box, a check mark appears in the check box, and PowerPoint turns the feature on. You turn a check box off by clicking it again to remove the check mark.

"Click to add text"   Placeholder text that appears on a slide to indicate where you can enter text. If you click this placeholder, a dotted outline box appears on-screen for you to type your text in.

Clipboard   A Windows feature in which your programs temporarily store information that you've copied or cut. In most cases, you can paste information into your slide from the Clipboard as many times as you want until you place new data on the Clipboard.

column   In a table, the vertical division of the text or numbers.

copy   To duplicate text or objects. When you copy an item, your program places the copy on the Windows Clipboard, and the original item remains intact.

cut   To remove text or objects from their original locations. When you cut an item, PowerPoint removes the original item and places it on the Clipboard.

Glossary

data Numbers or text you enter into a table or chart.

datasheet The table into which you enter your chart data.

default A setting or option that PowerPoint uses if you don't choose something else. When you select a command or open a dialog box, the setting or option that's already selected is the default. Usually, it's the choice most people are likely to make. If you want to choose something other than the default choice, you have to specify it in the dialog box.

demote To indent a text line more so that it appears in a less prominent position in the slide show outline.

design template One of a series of pre-designed slide designs that include colors, patterns, fonts, and formatting.

double-click To click the left mouse button twice quickly. In a dialog box, double-clicking a button is the same as clicking the button and clicking OK.

drag-and-drop A method you can use to move selected information from one location to another without going through the cut-and-paste process; drag-and-drop is much faster and more efficient. When you use this feature, you see the drag-and-drop mouse pointer.

Drawing toolbar A set of buttons you can use to draw objects such as lines, arrowheads, circles, and rectangles.

format To assign characteristics to text, paragraphs, charts, pages, and so on. For example, you can apply bold formatting to make text stand out more.

Formatting toolbar The second toolbar on the PowerPoint screen (under the Standard toolbar). This toolbar contains buttons you can use to format characters in slides by changing fonts and font sizes, applying bold, and changing the alignment of characters (to name a few).

graph *See* chart.

handles Small squares that surround an object or text block when you select it. You can click on a handle and drag it to resize the object or text block.

Help The menu whose commands you can use to access the online Help system, which contains information on a variety of subjects.

I-beam The standard mouse pointer's appearance when it is in a text block. When you see this mouse pointer (which looks like a capital letter I), you can enter or edit text at that position. If you want to move it somewhere else, just click on that spot.

justification The alignment of text relative to the left and right margins. When you justify text, PowerPoint inserts spaces of varying sizes between the words so that every line in the paragraph has the same width.

label Text or numbers (such as years or corporate departments) that you do not use for calculations.

legend Text and a sample pattern, symbol, or color you can use to show how you represent data in a chart. A legend is usually in a box.

logo Text or artwork that symbolizes a company or product. Advertising campaigns use logos frequently to inspire name recognition with a product. Companies often use logos as "brand marks" for their products or services. You can use the WordArt program to insert a logo on your slides.

Meeting Minder A feature that enables you to create Action Items and Meeting Minutes. The Meeting Minder records information from individual slides and saves the information within the presentation. You can then print out Meeting Minutes (using Microsoft Word for Windows if you like). Meeting Minder places your Action Items on a new slide that it adds to the end of the presentation, which can also be printed out.

Meeting Minutes   Information that you record during a presentation about individual slides.

menu   A list of commands from which you can choose. The File menu, for example, contains file-related commands such as Open, Close, and Exit.

menu bar   The horizontal strip near the top of the screen that contains available menus (which contain commands).

Notes Pages view   The view you use to add or display your slide notes. Notes Pages view can contain a thumbnail (small picture of a slide), and a text box into which you enter your note.

object   A text block or graphic image that you can move, copy, or resize. When you click an object once, handles surround the object. These handles enable you to resize or move the item.

Office Assistant   The on-call help system. Type a question into the Office Assistant's text box, and he'll look up an appropriate answer in the help system.

option button   An element (usually in a dialog box) that you use to make a selection. Click an option button to choose the corresponding option. You can select only one option button at a time; PowerPoint automatically deselects the previously selected button when you select a new one.

organization chart   A diagram that you use to illustrate the structure of a group of people. To use this feature, you need to install Microsoft Organization Chart (which comes with PowerPoint) on your computer.

Outline view   Shows each slide and its details without the graphics. You can collapse or expand information in slides depending on how much information you want to see. Using the Outline toolbar buttons, you can promote or demote slides by changing the amount of indentation used within slides, and you can change the order of slides within the presentation.

paste   To place the contents of the Clipboard in a new location.

placeholder   Dummy text or boxes that you replace with text, a table, a chart, or a graphic image. AutoLayout slides come with placeholders that you can replace with your own information.

presentation   The body of work you create in PowerPoint, which consists of one or more slides and other materials you use to assist you in a giving a speech. PowerPoint considers a "presentation" to be made up of both the file that contains your slides and the physical act of presenting the slides to a group of people.

promote   To indent a text line less so that the line is more prominent in your slide show outline.

recolor   To change the colors in a clip art image.

Redo   A command that enables you to reverse the last action or command on which you used the Undo command. You can also use Redo to repeat a command you just used.

resize   To change the size of an object by selecting it and dragging one of its handles.

save   In order to use your work at a later date, you need to store it within your computer (on your hard disk or on a floppy diskette).

scroll bars   Gray horizontal and vertical bars that appear on-screen and in dialog boxes and drop-down lists, usually along the edge of the screen or at the edge of the item in the dialog box or list. Scroll bars enable you to see screen areas or choices that are hidden from view. Scroll bars appear only when there is more information available than is visible on-screen.

select   To choose an object or text so that PowerPoint knows what you want to work with. Click on an object or text block to select it, and handles appear around the item. In most cases, you must select text or an object before you can move, copy, edit, or resize it.

slide   Each independent idea within a presentation comprises a slide. Each slide appears on your computer monitor in the shape of a 35mm slide (even if you don't create 35mm slides for your presentation).

Slide Show view   The view in which all the slides in the presentation, including transitions, animation effects, hidden slides, and text builds, appear on-screen. During a slide show, each slide fills the screen, and no menus or toolbars appear. You can show slide shows manually by controlling the show with your mouse or automatically so that PowerPoint shows the slides in a continuous loop until you press the Esc key.

Slide Sorter view   The view that shows all the slides in your presentation in miniature versions. You can use this view to apply transitions and reorganize the slides.

Slide view   Shows a single slide on your computer screen. This is the view you use to work with the clip art and the details of the individual slides.

sort   To change the order of information in a table. You can sort information alphabetically or numerically and in ascending or descending order.

Speaker's Notes   Your comments that appear on the Notes Pages. These notes can be as formal or informal as you want. Speaker's Notes basically replace the index cards you may have used in previous presentations.

Spelling Checker   A feature that searches your slides for misspellings. Check spelling using the Spell Check button on the Standard toolbar.

Standard toolbar   The first toolbar on the PowerPoint screen (it appears below the title bar at the top of your screen). This toolbar contains buttons you can use to perform common tasks such as saving and opening a file, printing, and checking spelling.

style   A preformatted arrangement of groups within an organization chart.

table   Information that you organize in columns and rows so you can present it in a way that is easy to read and understand. You must have Microsoft Word for Windows installed on your computer to create tables in PowerPoint.

Table AutoFormat   A feature that adds predesigned formatting to tables. Each Table AutoFormat includes borders, colors, patterns, and formatting.

text block   A box in which you enter and edit text. Each "Click to add text" placeholder is a text block.

three-dimensional   *See* 3-D.

thumbnail   A miniature view of a slide or design template. A thumbnail gives you an idea of what your slide looks like, but it is probably too small to actually read.

transition   An effect that determines how one slide advances to the next during a slide show. You can apply a different transition to each slide in your presentation.

Undo   A command that enables you to reverse a previous action. The Standard toolbar contains an Undo button.

views   Ways in which PowerPoint enables you to examine the information in your presentation. PowerPoint views include Outline, Slide, Slide Sorter, Notes Pages, and Slide Show. You switch between views using the buttons to the left of the horizontal scroll bar (in the lower-left corner of the screen).

WordArt   A feature that transforms text into interesting shapes. With WordArt, you can use different fonts, colors, and shadows to create text for a corporate logo.

X-axis   The horizontal reference line in a chart.

Y-axis   The vertical reference line in a chart.

Z-axis   In a 3-D chart, the z-axis represents the reference line that gives the chart its depth; the reference line goes from front to back.

Index

Index

S

Check out Que® Books on the World Wide Web
http://www.mcp.com/que

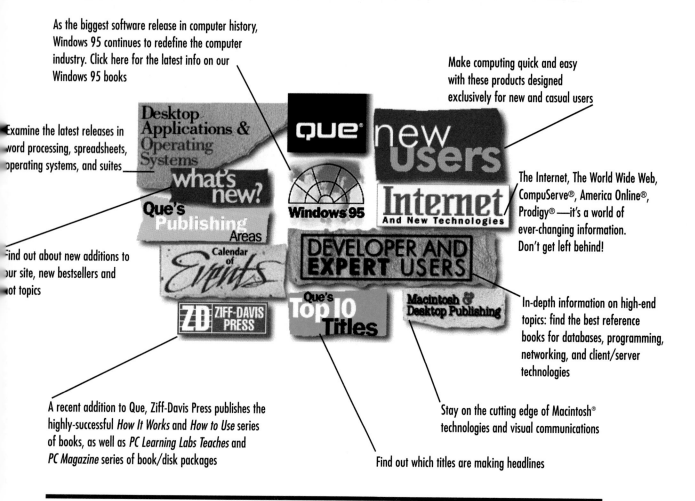

As the biggest software release in computer history, Windows 95 continues to redefine the computer industry. Click here for the latest info on our Windows 95 books

Make computing quick and easy with these products designed exclusively for new and casual users

Examine the latest releases in word processing, spreadsheets, operating systems, and suites

The Internet, The World Wide Web, CompuServe®, America Online®, Prodigy® —it's a world of ever-changing information. Don't get left behind!

Find out about new additions to our site, new bestsellers and hot topics

In-depth information on high-end topics: find the best reference books for databases, programming, networking, and client/server technologies

A recent addition to Que, Ziff-Davis Press publishes the highly-successful *How It Works* and *How to Use* series of books, as well as *PC Learning Labs Teaches* and *PC Magazine* series of book/disk packages

Stay on the cutting edge of Macintosh® technologies and visual communications

Find out which titles are making headlines

With 6 separate publishing groups, Que develops products for many specific market segments and areas of computer technology. Explore our Web Site and you'll find information on best-selling titles, newly published titles, upcoming products, authors, and much more.

- Stay informed on the latest industry trends and products available
- Visit our online bookstore for the latest information and editions
- Download software from Que's library of the best shareware and freeware

Complete and Return this Card
for a *FREE* Computer Book Catalog

Thank you for purchasing this book! You have purchased a superior computer book written expressly for your needs. To continue to provide the kind of up-to-date, pertinent coverage you've come to expect from us, we need to hear from you. Please take a minute to complete and return this self-addressed, postage-paid form. In return, we'll send you a free catalog of all our computer books on topics ranging from word processing to programming and the internet.

Mr. ☐   Mrs. ☐   Ms. ☐   Dr. ☐

Name (first) ☐☐☐☐☐☐☐☐☐☐☐☐   (M.I.) ☐   (last) ☐☐☐☐☐☐☐☐☐☐☐☐☐☐☐☐☐☐☐

Address ☐☐☐☐☐☐☐☐☐☐☐☐☐☐☐☐☐☐☐☐☐☐☐☐☐☐☐☐☐☐☐

City ☐☐☐☐☐☐☐☐☐☐☐☐☐☐☐☐   State ☐☐   Zip ☐☐☐☐☐ ☐☐☐☐

Phone ☐☐☐ ☐☐☐ ☐☐☐☐   Fax ☐☐☐ ☐☐☐ ☐☐☐☐

Company Name ☐☐☐☐☐☐☐☐☐☐☐☐☐☐☐☐☐☐☐☐☐☐☐☐☐☐☐☐

E-mail address ☐☐☐☐☐☐☐☐☐☐☐☐☐☐☐☐☐☐☐☐☐☐☐☐☐☐☐☐

1. Please check at least (3) influencing factors for purchasing this book.

Front or back cover information on book .... ☐
Special approach to the content .... ☐
Completeness of content .... ☐
Author's reputation .... ☐
Publisher's reputation .... ☐
Book cover design or layout .... ☐
Index or table of contents of book .... ☐
Price of book .... ☐
Special effects, graphics, illustrations .... ☐
Other (Please specify): _____ ☐

2. How did you first learn about this book?

Saw in Macmillan Computer Publishing catalog .... ☐
Recommended by store personnel .... ☐
Saw the book on bookshelf at store .... ☐
Recommended by a friend .... ☐
Received advertisement in the mail .... ☐
Saw an advertisement in: _____ ☐
Read book review in: _____ ☐
Other (Please specify): _____ ☐

3. How many computer books have you purchased in the last six months?

This book only .... ☐   3 to 5 books....................... ☐
2 books .... ☐   More than 5 .... ☐

4. Where did you purchase this book?

Bookstore .... ☐
Computer Store .... ☐
Consumer Electronics Store .... ☐
Department Store .... ☐
Office Club .... ☐
Warehouse Club .... ☐
Mail Order .... ☐
Direct from Publisher .... ☐
Internet site .... ☐
Other (Please specify): _____ ☐

5. How long have you been using a computer?

☐ Less than 6 months   ☐ 6 months to a year
☐ 1 to 3 years   ☐ More than 3 years

6. What is your level of experience with personal computers and with the subject of this book?

	With PCs	With subject of book
New	☐	☐
Casual	☐	☐
Accomplished	☐	☐
Expert	☐	☐

Source Code ISBN: 0-7897-0961-9

7. Which of the following best describes your job title?

Administrative Assistant .... ☐
Coordinator .... ☐
Manager/Supervisor .... ☐
Director .... ☐
Vice President .... ☐
President/CEO/COO .... ☐
Lawyer/Doctor/Medical Professional .... ☐
Teacher/Educator/Trainer .... ☐
Engineer/Technician .... ☐
Consultant .... ☐
Not employed/Student/Retired .... ☐
Other (Please specify): _____ ☐

8. Which of the following best describes the area of the company your job title falls under?

Accounting .... ☐
Engineering .... ☐
Manufacturing .... ☐
Operations .... ☐
Marketing .... ☐
Sales .... ☐
Other (Please specify): _____ ☐

Comments: _____
_____
_____

9. What is your age?

Under 20 .... ☐
21-29 .... ☐
30-39 .... ☐
40-49 .... ☐
50-59 .... ☐
60-over .... ☐

10. Are you:

Male .... ☐
Female .... ☐

11. Which computer publications do you read regularly? (Please list)

_____
_____
_____
_____
_____
_____
_____
_____
_____
_____

Fold here and scotch-tape to mail.

QUE'S MICROSOFT® OFFICE 97 RESOURCE CENTER

For the most up-to-date information about all the Microsoft Office 97 products, visit Que's Web Resource Center at

http://www.mcp.com/que/msoffice

The web site extends the reach of this Que book by offering you a rich selection of supplementary content.

You'll find information about Que books as well as additional content about these new **Office 97 topics**:

- **Word**
- **Excel**
- **PowerPoint®**
- **Visual Basic® for Applications**
- **Access**
- **Outlook™**
- **FrontPage™**

Visit Que's web site regularly for a variety of new and updated Office 97 information.

The best resources and tips for getting things done with Office 97!